CW00588423

THE VOICE

THE
VOICE

MY STORY
RAY WARREN
WITH ANDREW WEBSTER

NERO

Published by Nero,
an imprint of Schwartz Publishing Pty Ltd
37–39 Langridge Street
Collingwood VIC 3066 Australia
email: enquiries@blackincbooks.com
http://www.nerobooks.com.au

The National Library of Australia Cataloguing-in-Publication entry:

Warren, Ray, author.
The voice : my story / Ray Warren, with Andrew Webster.
9781863956758 (hardback)
9781922231796 (ebook)
Warren, Ray.
Sportscasters—Australia—Biography.
Sports journalism—Australia.
Webster, Andrew, author.
070.449796092

Cover design: Peter Long
Cover and author photographs courtesy of the Nine Network

CONTENTS

FOREWORD

BY ALAN JONES

I cannot remember when I first met Ray Warren, but I can remember my first impressions. He will think I'm gilding the lily a little when I say that every meeting with Ray Warren is an expression of his modesty about his own ability and of his interest in yours.

There are characteristics in sport which either commend people to you or discourage you from an association with them. This is because sport, and especially rugby league, is about more than what happens out there on the field.

In other words, there is more to a broadcaster than the person behind the microphone and the voice. Ray Warren would have become just one of the many broadcasters who plied their trade in many sporting fields, were it not for the fact that his fundamental decency has lifted him above and beyond others.

When it comes to rugby league commentary, there is little dispute that Ray Warren is the best in the business. What follows in these pages, though, explains more than that. It explains the ebb and flow of a career in the media. Amid the funny tales of gambling and socialising, this is a comeback story, as much as anything else.

From the age of six, Ray grew up wanting to call sport. He heard Ken Howard calling the horseracing on the wireless at home in Junee. You see, Ray Warren is a bushie. Ray Warren fell in love with racing. Like many of us, he fell in love with the artistry of Ken Howard, his colour and his accuracy, and in this way Ray very much fell in love with broadcasting.

Ray's cards were marked straight away: he was going to be a racecaller. And as the basis for his art he made phantom calls with marbles rolling down the hallway of his parents' home.

From there, he walked an unlikely path, from working on the railways to being a policeman in Canberra, to calling rugby league for 2LF in Young, to finally getting his start with 2GB, where he was understudy to Ken Howard and the comparable Johnny Tapp, calling the horse and harness racing.

He also started calling rugby league for 2GB from the

card table on the sidelines, alongside the likes of the legendary Frank Hyde and 'Tiger' Black.

But then television beckoned. Ray Warren became the voice of the Amco Cup for Channel Ten, and then gravitated towards full-time TV. He was set to anchor Channel Ten's coverage of the 1984 Los Angeles Olympics, but his deep fear of flying forced him to pull out.

I well remember, during my first year coaching Balmain, how we were to play a preseason game in Darwin. Ray was to broadcast the match for Channel Nine, and we were seated next to one another on the plane. He was a nervous wreck. I used to think the expression 'white knuckles' was an exaggeration – Ray Warren's whole body was white!

But in all of this, there was always a sense of humour. When I subsequently told the story about his genuine fear, his retort was: 'How would you know? From the moment the plane took off, your head went down like a beaten favourite and you fell asleep.'

The racing images were never far from his lips. And the tone of Ken Howard in his voice was equally never far away.

But his decision to resist flying eventually counted against him, and he was told: 'If you can't travel, you can't broadcast.' And so he was forced out.

He meandered around regional and country racetracks for
the next six years, before calling swimming for Channel Nine,
alongside Norman May, at the 1990 Commonwealth Games.
That opened the door for his return to rugby league. And,
as we all know, he is now as much a part of the fabric of the
game as any other figure, and that includes the players. We
can picture the iconic plays and epic moments in our minds,
but we can also hear them in stereo, in Ray Warren's voice.

To me, one of his extraordinary strengths is that he never
sets himself up as an authority on the game. His exchanges with
his 'expert commentators' are colourful and always without
malice. And, always aware that you can't play first-grade
rugby league without having ability, Ray Warren is never
judgemental about the people providing the entertainment
on the paddock.

He is forever mindful that without them, he has no job.
That is the inherent modesty of the man. In his field, he is
brilliant. But he never talks about it. He talks about the glory
of the game. The broadcaster, to Ray, always seems incidental.

I remember a couple of years ago when Ray was diagnosed
with prostate cancer, a frightening reality which is faced
by many men. I've been down that track too. As soon as
I heard, I phoned Ray and told him there was only one

man he needed to speak to: Dr Phil Stricker at St Vincent's Hospital in Sydney.

Ray was nervous and apprehensive, so I sought to reassure him. I simply told him that all he had to do was to turn up – let Phil Stricker do the rest. Ray was forever grateful. He's that kind of bloke.

That might also be why he has come through the other side of that ordeal and continues to call sport like no other. Indeed, much like Richie Benaud, he is universally loved in an unforgiving industry, and in the sometimes merciless world of sport. I often wonder, as do others, what will we do without him, because Ray Warren is the enduring voice of rugby league.

I know you'll enjoy his story. It is, as I have said, apart from anything else, a comeback story; a story of talent born with modesty; a story of decency and humility. But for me, above all else, it is the story of yet another boy from the bush made good.

The sporting world will always acknowledge that, whenever a discussion about great sporting broadcasters takes place, there will be mention made of Ray Warren. There can be no greater legacy.

Alan Jones AO
April 2014

PREFACE

BY ANDREW WEBSTER

I was the one. I was the annoying kid sitting tall on the back seat of the school bus, driving all within earshot mad with my impersonation of Ray 'Rabbits' Warren . . .

'Ohh! Crunching tackle from Gillespie! Dead-set drives him back about two metres!'

'Yeah, I've had that one replayed to me before,' says Rabs. 'I don't know where this stuff comes from. It just comes out.'

I was the one. I was the annoying teenager sitting tall in the back row of the classroom, driving the teacher and everyone else mad with my Rabs impersonation . . .

'And now for Steven Menzies! Ohh! Shut the gate! He'll run out of Brookvale!'

'Yeah, he'll run out of the stadium,' says Rabs. 'He'll run out of Brookvale. There are things in me that just come out.'

And I was the one, standing tall with my mates at the university bar, peeling off another impersonation of Rabs straight from that weekend's matches . . .

'*Kick and chase by Mullins! Kick and chase again by Mullins! This will be a miracle. Ohh! It is a miracle! Oh my goodness! You won't see anything like that again this year – and maybe never!*'

'Jesus, and what a try that was,' enthuses Rabs, without fail, every time I remind him of the try by Canberra fullback Brett Mullins against Brisbane on a freezing Friday night at Bruce Stadium in 1995.

And now here I am, standing behind Ray Warren as he takes his seat in the cramped Channel Nine commentary box at the back of Allianz Stadium. Tonight's fixture: the 2013 Preliminary Final between the Sydney Roosters and the Newcastle Knights. The possibility for a fairytale is everywhere, as each side tries to grab the last ticket to the Grand Final against Manly the following weekend.

'Are you nervous, Rabs?' I ask. He's been calling headline matches such as this one for the best part of four decades, for radio and television, for different paymasters and for an audience spanning several generations.

'Yes,' he says. 'I'm getting more nervous as I get older –
for lots of reasons.'

The Roosters are favourites. They have the bionic Sonny
Bill Williams, and have breezed through the past month
towards a premiership which, less than a year earlier, few had
predicted them to win. But things have got weird lately. The
team has been battered in the media for the past four days,
with front-page headlines concerning the elevated levels of
human growth hormone of some of their players after the
information was found on a crime figure's mobile phone.
Very weird, but very rugby league.

In the visitors' dressing room stands the angular figure of
Wayne Bennett, who has taken all of his 35 years as a coach,
his seven premierships and his countless finals appearances, and
injected it into a Knights side that didn't look like reaching
the finals series a month ago, let alone making it to the Big
Dance. Bennett doesn't have Sonny Bill but he does have
Danny Buderus, the 35-year-old hooker and ornament of
the game, who will retire as soon as the Knights lose.

Perhaps like no other sport, rugby league understands
theatre. The game's soap opera thrives on scandal and hype
and magnification, and when it comes to match day –
especially the really *big* match days – there is no other

individual who allows it to crackle and fizz like the best caller in the business.

Rabs takes his seat in the middle of the panel, and slips on the headphones and microphone that have his name written on them in texta. To the right of him is Peter Sterling. To the left is Phil Gould. The three of them have clocked hundreds of games together. They are about to call the biggest game of the season so far, but are as calm as three men sitting at the bar. Rabs starts them off . . .

'Welcome back to Allianz Stadium, and the atmosphere here is unbelievable . . .'

When Rabs calls football matches, he's like a percolating volcano. He builds, slowly, waiting for the right time to erupt, and on this night the moment comes with six minutes and 42 seconds on the clock. Roosters five-eighth James Maloney comes within inches of scoring, only to be denied by the left upright, the turf, and two desperate Newcastle defenders.

'Maloney's close! But that's as close as he's gonna get!'

Until this point, Sterling has made several routine remarks but Gould has not offered a syllable. An hour before kickoff, I was sitting with the three-time premiership-winning coach in the back row of the western grandstand, in front of the broadcast boxes. It was clear that the last place he wanted to be was Allianz Stadium.

'How are you, Gus?' I asked.

'Miserable,' he said without emotion, running a cranky eye over the players below as they warm up. 'I haven't slept and I'm on painkillers.'

For everything he's accomplished, for all the premierships and Origin series victories and his resurrection of the embattled Penrith Panthers, rugby league exhausts Gould. After plopping down in his seat in the commentary box about twenty minutes before kickoff, he gets the attention of the assistant, Louise.

'Lou, I'm not going to make it if you don't get me a bottle of Coke,' he tells her. 'And some chips . . . Have you asked him if he wants some chips?' Gould points at long-time statistician David Middleton, who doesn't want any chips. 'I'll have a pie, too,' says Gould, completing the pre-match order.

The most commonly asked question of the Channel Nine rugby league commentary team is whether Ray Warren and Phil Gould like each other. They squabble like an old married couple – or perhaps like Statler and Waldorf from *The Muppet Show* – and thousands of viewers are unsure if the arguments and vaudeville and raised voices are genuine.

'Oh, yeah,' says Rabs. 'It's the most oft asked question I get: "Do you and Gus really not get on?" And I have to say, "No, I get on fine with him. I love him." I have so many people say to me, "Don't let him get on top of you."'

Gould loves Rabs, too. He once wrote an entire column for the *Sydney Morning Herald* about his head caller's palpable fear of climbing into a helicopter so they could attend a game on the Gold Coast. The kickoff was delayed to accommodate their late arrival after a delay in their flight from Sydney. 'Wow,' Gould told him. 'Holding the game up for you, Rabbits. That's huge.'

'He's one of the strangest people I've ever met in my life, you know,' says Rabs of his expert caller. 'He knows I refer to him as not bipolar but tripolar, because I think I've seen three Guses in the one day. In the commentary box there's nobody better than Gus. But the ritual. That's weird. He sits there and he eats a bucket of chips and he drinks a Coke, and it's normally about the seventh minute of the game when he comes in and says something. And it might be an innocuous comment like, "Isn't this just fantastic, Rabbits? Sunday football – don't people love their Sunday football?" Yeah, Gus, you've said that before. We all love our Sunday football. Yeah, good.'

With his pie and the chips devoured, and everything

washed down by half a bottle of Coke, Gould springs to life.

'Wow!' he shouts as Maloney is stopped inches short of the tryline. 'Well, the Newcastle Knights have come up with a couple of real try-savers in the first six and a half minutes on their own tryline. Maloney looked certain to score. Absolutely certain to score.'

For the next 74 minutes, this is how it plays out. Rabs views the match through the same binoculars he's used to watch sport for decades. The Carl Zeiss 10x50s he's had since the 1970s. 'They've been my trusted friend for so long,' he explains. Andrew Johns once dropped them, and they had to be put back into alignment.

In the 17th minute, Danny Buderus races up to tackle Jared Waerea-Hargreaves, and his head accidentally clashes with the left elbow of the giant Roosters prop. He is knocked out cold. The broadcast goes to a commercial break and Rabs picks it up when it returns.

'Danny Buderus is about to be placed on a stretcher and then onto the medicab. This is the last thing anyone in football, anyone in sport, wanted to see as the departure of Danny Buderus.'

He glances down at a sheet of paper in front of him, on which are some notes about Buderus. On most occasions for Rabs the words 'just come out', but sometimes he needs to be prepared.

'He came from Taree, 17 years ago,' he observes. '257 NRL games, 24 Tests, 21 Origins . . .'

The first try of the match is scored by Roosters winger Daniel Tupou from a cross-field kick in which he leaps high above his Knights opposite, Akuila Uate. Rabs describes the action in his unique way.

'*Up goes Tupou, with the football . . . There's the first try of the night, scored by Daniel Tupou! Six-foot-three in the old language. He jumped three feet off the ground. What hope did Akuila have, short of a ladder?*'

In the final minute of the first half, the Roosters concede a penalty, stripping the ball from Knights centre Dane Gagai.

'It's a stupid rule,' Rabs fumes. 'I hate it.'

'You hate that rule, don't you, Rabbits?' asks Gus, playfully.

'I hate it! It lacks common sense.'

'I can see that,' Gus grins at the rest of us in the back of the commentary box. 'Any time you're standing up, I know you hate something.' We can all see that, in fact, the head caller hasn't moved from his seat.

For as long as he could remember, as a youngster growing up in the Riverina town of Junee, Rabs wanted to be a horserace caller. That was where he realised the value of 'light and shade', and as the Roosters build on their half-time lead, he uses healthy doses of both.

'Akuila Uate, I love him. Love his personality. Here's Jennings! Jennings is away! Here comes another try!'

Then, as the Knights mount a spirited comeback late in the game, he explodes again.

'A Tyrone Roberts Knights kick. It's very much a Hail Mary – but she's answered the prayers of BJ Leilua! He's scored again!'

When Roosters backrower Aidan Guerra scores a try in the dying minute, it gives Statler and Waldorf one last chance to do their thing.

'Guerra . . . Where does that come from?' Rabs asks.

'French, I think,' says Gus.

'I would've thought Italian. It ends in a vowel.'

'Well, I didn't know I had to sit for an exam here tonight.'

'Well, I didn't know you were asking for the Holden Cup score again.'

'Well, who won Holden Cup?'

'The Panthers won easily, and you know that. I don't know if it's an ad for Penrith or Holden . . . *The try is converted and, ladies and gentleman, there is no more. And these men from Bondi, from the junction and the beach, will come back again next*

Sunday to play Manly for the crown. They call it the Big Dance. Well, the Roosters are gonna dance with the Eagles.'

Now that the match is over, it's time for Rabs to activate the exit strategy that has become legendary. On this night, there's a limousine waiting on Moore Park Road. As he walks through the buzzing crowd, down through the members and out towards the car park, fans stare. 'Look! It's Rabs!' says one. A middle-aged man in a Roosters jumper stops in his tracks and breaks into applause. 'Irreplaceable!' he bellows.

As Rabs makes his way down the steps, a seven-year-old boy spots the 70-year-old caller, who is always heard but rarely seen on television. The kid's eyes light up like he's just bumped into Sonny Bill, and he sticks up his hand, which Rabs gladly high fives.

Eventually, we make it to the limo. 'Before you go, Rabs,' I say, 'tell me why you were nervous? Alongside Gus and Sterlo, you piloted the coverage like you were steering the *Starship Enterprise.'*

He laughs. 'I think I've got a reasonable reputation, and I've worked hard at that,' he says. 'I mean, I didn't want to be a failure. I always wanted to be successful, and I think I enjoy that success now. The last thing I want to do is to stuff it up, and that's what worries me, as I get older.

'Sometimes, when you get old, you make mistakes and you don't know you're making them. It's called senility. It's the onset of possible dementia, and I've worked with a couple of commentators who were in that stage. It's okay to make a mistake as long as you know you've made it, because then you can correct it, but if you're making mistakes and you don't know you've made them . . . There are only a few people close to me who I want to be telling me that I've reached that point. Whenever I go to work, that's on my mind.'

As I think about this, he continues speaking.

'Everybody's replaceable. Whoever replaces me probably won't have the sayings that I've got, and he mightn't have the voice that I've got, but I'm very replaceable. Once you start thinking you're indispensable, then you probably make yourself hugely dispensable. I've been there before.'

Ray Warren's story is like many others in the realm of sport, regardless of which side of the commentary box glass you find yourself on: a young kid from the bush, chasing a dream that takes him to the city, before he loses it all and finds it again. Along the way, however, Rabs became a household name. The best caller in the business. The Voice.

Andrew Webster
April 2014

1

BEGINNINGS

To understand my story, you need to know where all this started. I think it will help you appreciate who I am if you know something about the humble background I come from. As you'll see, I definitely wasn't born with a silver spoon in my mouth.

When I was a boy in the late 1940s, my family lived in a little three-bedroom weatherboard house in Junee, New South Wales. It was a falling-down sort of a house, if you know what I mean. Ours was a big family, so I didn't have my own bedroom. We had to double up, or sometimes it was three to a room. I was the only one of the family born in Junee – all the others were born in Coolamon.

We had no hot water, and Mum cooked everything on

or in the wood stove. That stove was almost the centrepiece of our entire home. There was always a pot of tea brewing on the hotplate, and you could use a long fork to make your toast off the embers for brekky. The stove was where we heated water to do the washing up, and so Dad could have a shave. And it was where everyone wanted to warm their bum!

We had no refrigerator – we made do with an ice chest. A man used to come around selling blocks of ice, which went into the chest to keep things cool. Bread and milk were delivered by horse and cart.

In the bathroom there was no shower, only a bath. We probably bathed a couple of times a week and had a 'bird bath' on the other days. Our bathwater was heated by a special boiler, which also kept the bathroom wonderfully warm. Its fuel was woodchips – the scraps from the wood Dad chopped every day for the stove.

To do the washing, Mum would fill a wood-fired copper with water and toss in the clothes. There was no spin dryer; Mum would wring out the clothes by hand and then hang them on a clothesline in the backyard. We only had an outside dunny, and in winter that was as cold as it gets! Redbacks under the seat and all that.

We had no car – our mode of transport was by pushbike or on foot. There was no telephone and of course no television. Our entertainment centred on the kitchen: that was where we ate, and we often played board games and listened to the radio there too. We had no dining room or lounge room as such.

Dad was a fettler working on the railway lines. Mum, as well as looking after all of us, cleaned the bank and the courthouse in Junee, and at one time cooked at one of the hotels. Dad mended our shoes, and Mum darned our socks. Today, we throw those things away.

Being born during the Second World War as the youngest of seven children had some drawbacks. The same year I was born, my eldest brother, Jack, went on active duty. The year before that, my eldest sister, Gwen, got married, and her husband Bert also went off to the war. My sisters June and Betty both got married when I was very young, so that took them away from the family home as well. I was about eight years old when my youngest sister, Val, also tied the knot.

So the only one of my brothers and sisters that I remember really well from when I was young is my brother Bob. I looked up to him greatly. He was my protector on many occasions, and took me with him just about everywhere he went. I can still hear Mum saying, 'Bob, where are you going? Don't go without Ray.' One thing we loved was rabbiting. He'd put me on his shoulders and off we'd go, with a pick and a shovel and our dog.

Later in life, Bob joined the police force, and he even won the Queen's award for bravery. It was his influence that would see me join the police force too. Bob also played President's Cup for Canterbury, then made grade with Newtown before going back to the country, where he was captain-coach of Eden-Monaro a couple of times in the 1960s.

A second influence of the war at that time was that my parents never got me baptised, so I was never properly christened. That never bothered me as much as it bothered them. But it did present a problem when I applied to join the police force and was told I needed a baptismal certificate.

So off I went to the Presbyterian church at Paddington – I was boarding in Paddo at the time – and I met the minister there and told him my story. He gave me some information to read and told me to come back the next day. 'We'll do it then,' he said.

When I showed up the next day, we got started. I'll never forget the first question he asked me: 'So what do you want to call yourself?'

'What do you mean?' I said.

'What Christian names do you want? You can change what you've got, if you like.'

Funnily enough, I really hated my second name, Eric. *Here's my chance to get rid of Eric forever!* I thought. But then my regard for Mum and Dad's wishes took over, so I said: 'Just leave me as I am. I'll make do with what I've got.'

I've learnt a lot over my life, and these days, when I'm asked to speak at functions, I try to emphasise that it doesn't matter where you come from or how simple your existence might have been. All that matters is whether you have the passion, the desire, the energy and the persistence to chase your dreams. If you do, anything is possible. And that's the most important thing of all.

2

SACKED (NOT REALLY)

I learnt quickly that none of us should ever think we are indispensable.

It was 1986, and I was working for Channel Ten. I'd called all the station's rugby league broadcasts since 1974, including the midweek Amco Cup and then the Winfield Cup. After working for the station for that length of time, I suppose I had come to feel comfortable in my position. After all, no one had ever complained about the job I was doing. I felt pretty secure – but I was not. In fact, I was working on borrowed time, as I soon discovered.

In July of that year I was asked to come in to the network's offices, only to be told I wouldn't be calling the footy after the season had finished. Ten would be getting in Rex Mossop,

I was told. I'd received no warnings, nor had I even been told I could be doing better. Nothing at all.

'You can choose to go now or after the Grand Final,' they said. They offered me a job doing their racing – but Ten didn't have any racing!

I felt I had done nothing wrong, so I decided to stay on till the Grand Final. Parramatta beat Canterbury that year at the Sydney Cricket Ground, and it was the last match for Eels legends Ray Price and Mick Cronin. In my mind, I was retiring too. As I uttered my last words on air, I fell in a heap, broken-hearted.

I'm just a country kid who had a dream and saw it come true. I grew up beside a railway line near Junee, in the Riverina region of New South Wales, and from the age of six, from the moment I won money on the first horse I was allowed to have a bet on, hearing Ken Howard call it home on the radio, I knew what I wanted to do. I wanted to be a sports broadcaster.

In the early 1980s Ten had given me the best platform to do this. I'd called the Amco Cup as a freelancer for them in the mid 1970s, and then they made me sports director in 1978. I can honestly say that was the only time in my life when I hated TV.

John McEnroe was the final straw. I went out to Sydney Airport at 5.30 am one day, along with every other reporter, just to stick a microphone under his nose at a doorstop press conference. These were the days of film, and it took six hours to process a 40-second piece. So by about 5.30 pm – twelve hours later – I was getting my make-up on and my hair done, ready to go on air and read my five minutes of sports news, including the McEnroe story.

That night, I asked myself, 'What am I doing here? What am I doing this for? I hate it.' All I wanted to do was call live sport. I came off the news desk and wrote a note to the news director, Tom Barnett: 'Dear Tom, I don't like the job I'm doing. I need to leave.'

He phoned me the next day. 'There's no need to come in today,' he said. 'Don't worry about it.' I was gone.

A year later, Ten came calling again. I was standing in a bar at Lang Park, in Brisbane, when the station's general manager, Ian Kennon, approached me. 'What happened to us?' he asked.

'I didn't like the job,' I replied. 'I found out by doing that job that all I want to do is call sport. I don't want to report on it. I don't want airports, hair, make-up and all that bullshit.'

'Well, let's get married again,' said Ian. 'Let's get married again, and you just be our head presenter on major sport and call sport? Forget the news.'

Ten won the rights to the Winfield Cup the following year, and I finally had the job I had always wanted – right up to July 1986, when John Davies called me into his office. John was the production manager, and my best mate at the network.

'We've just renewed our contract with the league for the Winfield Cup for another three years,' he explained.

'Oh, that's fantastic, mate,' I said, elated.

'But you won't be doing it.'

'What?'

'They want Mossop. The network wants Mossop.'

'They want Mossop?'

'Yeah, because even though we think you're the best, they want him.'

'Well, it's a nice way of telling me!'

'Mossop's able to pull big figures on the news.'

Rex Mossop, known as 'The Moose'. The retired dual international and Manly legend who had called Sunday matches for Channel Seven, and had become an institution as a result. He'd been reading about fifteen minutes of sports news on Seven and it was rating well. Of course Ten wanted somebody with that gravitas.

As it happened, I'd worked with Rex on radio at 2GB and we'd never had cross words. I'd never bagged him. In fact, I'd always admired him and his work. I'd admired that attitude, that arrogance. It was aggressive, it was bombastic. There was only one opinion. I knew enough about commercial television to know that was a major plus. His appeal lay in his nature, in his knock-'em-down, drag-'em-out style. He was just like that on the news as well.

I'd never played to his level, but I knew within myself that I could call the game as well as anyone – including him.

The fact that Ten now wanted to replace me with Rex embarrassed me, but that had nothing to do with ego. I was frustrated that I couldn't put it all together. What bothered me the most was that my best mate, John Davies, had said, 'We think you're the best.' To me, the decision was so contradictory. If I was the best, why was I going out the door? I wished he'd put together a tape from the last twelve months and pointed out ten glaring mistakes that I'd made. That would have made things easier.

In the months that followed, I found out that there'd been clandestine meetings between Ten's management and

Rex, and that they'd been going on for quite some time. Years later, there were rumours that a particular individual working for Channel Ten also played a part in my demise, but I never gave any credence to that. To me, it was merely rumour. Other people might still talk about that, but I won't because I can't prove it.

After Davies had delivered the dreadful news in mid-1986, he said something that made the decision even more curious: 'You can go now or you can stay and do the Grand Final.'

It didn't make any sense. 'Well, you've made Mossop the offer,' I said. 'I've done nothing wrong, and I can't call any better than I'm calling. I'll stay and finish what I've started.'

In fairness, as I said, they did offer me the job of covering racing for the network. Racing? They didn't have any racing coming out of Sydney. That was the best Clayton's offer I've ever had.

So I called the 1986 Grand Final, trying desperately not to let my sadness affect my professionalism. As 'The Crow' and 'Pricey' did their lap of honour of the SCG, I put the microphone down and cried my eyes out. I was very hurt, and I was bitter about it. Then I was cut loose, set adrift out in no-man's-land for six years, a period of my life in which I lost control.

When I look back at it now, I see that this was also a time in my life when I learnt so much. More than anything, I learnt that you must never think that you're indispensable. Because nobody is. I learnt that the hardest way of all.

3

PLAYBOY

It all started, for better or worse, with a Playboy. He was the first horse I ever had a bet on, and he won, and that was the first time I knew exactly what I wanted to be. That's what prompted me, in my spare time, to roll marbles down a slope in the lounge room and call them as if they were racehorses. That was where this career of mine started, and it was brought about by a combination of accident and convenience.

I was six years old. It was 1949, and Dad was looking after me while Mum went to an auction to buy some galvanised iron for the roof, which had been leaking. I'd been sick with chickenpox and in bed for some time, and I was agitated and frustrated, like most kids would be at that age. It was a Saturday afternoon and, as usual, Dad was having his threepence or sixpence each-way bet on the races.

I managed to shake sixpence out of my sister Val's moneybox and, without too much persuasion, Dad agreed to let me have a bet with the SP bookmaker he placed all his wagers with. He was trying to shut me up so he could go through the day without my complaining. What happened next was incredible, however, and it changed everything.

I chose to put my money on the only racing name I'd ever heard of, the great jockey George Moore. It didn't matter to me what he was riding or the horse's form. I just knew how good he was, even at that tender age. As it turned out, I backed a horse in the AJC Derby at Randwick that had never won a race before. Anyone who knows racing will tell you a maiden winning a derby – which is a race open to three-year-old horses – is almost unheard of, even if the trainer was the legendary Tommy Smith.

But the unheard of happened. Playboy won the 1949 AJC Derby, and I backed it at 20 to 1 to win ten shillings. From that day on, Dad let me have an interest on the horses every weekend. Naturally, I only backed horses George Moore was riding, and most times they won.

I wish George had been able to ride forever, because with his retirement I went the way of most punters. I don't care what anyone tells you: whether you are gambling on horses or dogs or trots or whatever, unless you're in the know, unless you're getting the best mail, you can't win. In fact, even if you are in the know I still wonder if you can win more often than not.

To say I was hooked on the gamble at six years of age is not the case, but I was hooked on the voice we listened to on the radio. It became a fascination. That sound enveloped my existence, and the caller became my whole life.

He was so excited and passionate about the horses and about every race he described. He made it sound real to the listener out there who couldn't be at the track. He had sayings that printed an image in my mind that I just couldn't shake. *'Here comes the favourite with a wet sail . . . What's this at 100 miles an hour . . . This leader is heading for the line with his molars bared to the breeze . . . I'll bet London to a brick on that this has won . . . Don't bet odds-on and don't run up steps.'*

The voice belonged to Ken Howard, and even at that young age I knew I wanted to be just like him. I wanted to be a sports broadcaster. That was when I turned to the marbles. Until that time, I'd played with them like any kid did: big ring, little ring, no fudgin', play for keeps or for fun.

One day I accidentally knocked over my tin of marbles and they rolled down to the lowest point in our house. Suddenly I got an idea: they would be horses, and I would be Ken Howard! So each of the marbles became a horse, with its own colour and its own name.

Playboy was my favourite, of course. There were others, though, including San Domenico, Kingster, Knave, Dubbo, Baron Boissier, Benvolo and Dark Marne. Persian Lyric and Prince Darius came later, along with Turkestan and Dhaulagiri, Morse Code, Mac's Amber, Lord and Tulloch – the best horse ever.

I must have been around eight or nine when I started rolling the darn things and calling them like they were racing. We had a valve radio that was as big as a small refrigerator, and the more I called the rolling marbles, the more I tried to sound like the man's voice coming from it.

I built a horse out of a log of wood in the backyard. It became Playboy, and later Tulloch, and I made a saddle to soften the rough effect of sitting on a log. There I was, up the backyard, kicking home another winner and calling the race at the same time. It was fantastic. My horse never lost. When it was raining, I'd ride a broomstick around our smoke-filled kitchen. The smoke belonged to my dad, whom everyone knew as Old Joe. He loved nothing more than some Champion Ruby ready-rubbed tobacco, rolled up in a Tally-Ho.

Hardly a day went by when I didn't roll the marbles, ride the broomstick or sit on the wooden horse and boot home a winner, desperately trying to sound like Ken Howard. In the end, I probably sounded more like Ken Howard than Ken Howard himself.

My imagination was running wild. Junee was a little town of 3000 people. There was no radio station. There was no racecourse. There were no horses. There was no way I could call a real race or set myself up with a tripod and binoculars. I had nobody to turn to, but all I could hear was Ken Howard.

When he was calling a race, I could see these horses. I could see everything this man was saying to me. He was painting a picture with words, which is the art of radio, the art of sports broadcasting, and I could see the race in my mind.

He'd have a horse 'flashing down the outside at 100 miles an hour, underneath the roses'. *There are roses?* Now I could see roses growing on the outside fence of the racetrack. Horses would be 'travelling on a piece of cotton', or jockeys would be 'high in the irons', and I could see all these things. It fascinated me that Howard could turn these words into a picture.

I took an important lesson from all of this. If I ever got the chance to broadcast a race on the radio, then to be good at it — to be as good as Ken Howard — I had to pretend I was broadcasting to a blind man. I had to use my voice to tell the story.

★

I came out at 11 and a quarter pounds — a big bastard. Thankfully, Mum was a big woman of about 18 stone and she'd already had six children before me, so she had plenty of practice. Andrew Denton, the radio and TV star, once reckoned I was born as a walking, talking corpuscle. Peter Sterling said I had a head like the Japanese flag. Mum would not have liked that, let me tell you.

Contrary to the beliefs of Denton and Sterling, I was a normal-looking kid on arrival. The red face only caught up with me much later in life, and while it's been the butt of many jokes, it probably prolonged my career. Having this red melon means they don't put me on camera very much, so it's only my voice and audio performance that gets judged. I have a good head for radio, as they say.

So there I was. This enormous Rabbit came to life on

11 June 1943, although it took me a long time to grow. My nickname at school was 'Runty'.

People ask me where I got my voice. There is nobody in my family who sounds like me, with the exception of my eldest son, Mark. I didn't get my voice from my mother, but I reckon she gave me my sense of theatre.

If an event around town didn't have a compere, she'd compere it. If they didn't have somebody to sing 'God Save the Queen', she'd sing it. She had a beautiful voice. The voice of a lark. And if you wanted a bit of entertainment afterwards, she'd tell the dirtiest jokes that you could possibly think of. Our family was Christian, but even if there were clergymen in attendance Mum still told the jokes.

As I said, Mum was a big woman, although she wasn't tall, and she had a long-running battle with her weight. Dad wouldn't travel so Mum took me everywhere, including holidays at the People's Palace in Pitt Street, Sydney. It was owned for more than a century by the Salvation Army, and it provided very economical accommodation.

When you're being spoilt, you tend to have good times, and we did. I remember that in Sydney I wouldn't go to bed at night unless we jumped on a tram out the front and did the circuit – up to Central Railway Station, then down

Castlereagh Street then the Quay and back up Pitt Street, all while eating sixpence worth of cherries.

Mum would boil a billy in our room on a Primus stove fuelled by methylated spirits. She also used to cook our morning toast on it, gently stroking the bread over the flame.

She would take me on the ferry to the zoo and to Manly, and the boat would rock while we went past Sydney Heads. I always insisted that we stood in the middle to minimise the swaying. We would go to the races at Randwick or Rosehill and have a bonzer time.

Back in Junee, when storms struck, Mum would put me to bed with a bike tube; she believed the rubber would repel the lightning. If I scratched myself on a rose bush, it was off to the doctor's for a tetanus injection. She was petrified of rose bush injuries. She always made me check under the toilet seat for redbacks. My brother Jack was nearly killed by one that bit him on the bum several times. He was fairly slow.

Once a year we would head off to the railway picnic at Narrandera. I would always win the kids' footraces, and Mum would win the nail-driving competition. My God, she could use that hammer. With my running and her nail-driving, and all the first prizes she won at local shows for her scones, we made a little pocket money.

Mum was an incredible woman. She'd take the rifle and go out and bring back the evening meal. Later in life, she catered for weddings. She knew exactly what was required, right down to the last slice of meat or tomato or beetroot or onion. She did it all herself.

Mum always insisted we go to the toilet before bunking down for the night. It was an outside dunny, and she didn't like going alone. I remember one night in particular very well. She grabbed my hand and we charged off towards the loo at 100 miles an hour. At 18 stone, if you back down onto something as fragile as a toilet at any sort of speed, then anything's likely to happen. And on this night, it did.

Mum rushed in backwards, pulled the bloomers down and let everything go at the same time, including her robust frame. The toilet caved in. Water and other items came flooding out, along with fragments of the Royal Doulton. She started laughing uncontrollably. Dad had made the chain quite long so I could reach it. Mum reached up from where she was sitting and tried to pull herself up, and the waves and the gushing and the Royal Doulton and everything else came cascading out the door again.

Thank heavens she had a sense of humour. I will never forget Mum and the things she did. She had recipes in her head that no one could ever re-create. She had energy like you wouldn't believe, and the drive and the enthusiasm to make others just as passionate.

While Mum was an extrovert, Dad was the opposite. He was only small but tough as teak. He could have been in the clerical side of the railways, but no way. 'I'm not doing some pen-pusher's job, sitting on my arse all day,' he'd insist. So he took the alternative: a pick and shovel. He was a fettler, building and looking after the railway line.

Before I was born, Dad looked after a strip of railway line between Coolamon and Brushwood, about 40 kilometres north-west of Wagga Wagga. He was in charge of that line to make sure it didn't buckle or twist or fall into disrepair in any way. Mum's job was to raise six kids (I hadn't been born then), and at the same time to look after the weighbridge at the silo and the level-crossing gates.

All those little towns in the grain-producing areas of Australia had a railway line, a weighbridge and a silo. Whenever a bloke came through with a truck full of wheat, oats or whatever, or with a horse and cart full of the same, she'd put them across the weighbridge and weigh them, so they would eventually get paid for the amount of grain. She was the first woman in Australia, and maybe the only woman, ever to hold a weighbridge-man's licence. She was very proud of that.

Mum and Dad did all this while living in the railway humpy at Brushwood, near Junee: a little, falling-down, weatherboard house. To get anywhere, they would get on the railway trike, which was a three-wheeler with no motor, and manually drive it to wherever they wanted to go further down the line. They didn't have a supermarket next door. They would ride pushbikes or get on an occasional train to go into Junee to do their shopping, but mostly they lived off the fat of the land. They had a lot of chickens. Mum used to joke about the number of meals per week that were chicken – baked one night, casserole the next, curried the night after that. Dad didn't have to chop any heads off – a passing train did it for him. Rabbits and mushrooms were also a large part of the family's diet.

When I was a kid, we played lots of sport. Cricket, tennis, swimming, bike-hockey (my bike was my best friend), rugby league, Aussie Rules – you name it, we had a go. Tennis was my best, I suppose. I was chosen to represent the town at around the age of 13 at Wagga. They had assembled the champion boy and girl from each of the surrounding towns for a week of coaching under Vic Edwards, who was the bloke who discovered Evonne Goolagong.

At the end of the week, they played a knockout tournament to decide who would go to Sydney for the age championships. I won my first round and needed to win the round of eight or quarter final to progress to the big smoke. I'd never been beaten playing anyone at my own age. That was about to end.

I played this little leftie from Tarcutta. We were both small and could hardly see over the net. He thrashed me, the little bastard, and I was so disappointed that I gave the game away for a long time. Turned out the kid's name was Tony Roche, and he went on to win grand slams and coach the best players we've ever seen. Can you believe it?

Many years later, I met him through another great of the game, John Newcombe, who I worked with for several years while I was covering the tennis for Channel Ten.

One night Rochey came up to the box. I had told Newcombe how I'd played Roche and what it meant to me. So when Roche walked in, Newk said to him: 'Tony, do you remember Ray? You played him once in Wagga.'

'Never heard of him,' says Roche.

I was shattered – he didn't remember! How could he have forgotten? I knew he'd been to Wimbledon and the US and French Opens a thousand times, but how could he have forgotten Wagga in 1956!

★

I loved Dad when I was growing up, but Mum had spoilt me so I guess I was more attached to her. I was like Mum's handbag – she took me everywhere. One time in the mid-1940s we took a train over to Tumut, where my sister Gwen and her husband lived.

As it happened, Junee was challenging Tumut for the Maher Cup that weekend. And lo and behold, Junee won! There was great merriment afterwards, as Mum and I discovered when we got on the train for the journey home. The grog was flowing and the team and its supporters were jubilant.

From Tumut, the train came down the hills to Cootamundra, where the driver and the fireman had to take the engine off one end and put it on the other. As they were doing this, some larrikins locked them in the guard's van and took control of the train. Off we went for the final leg of the journey to Junee!

Sitting next to Mum and me was another woman who had gone to visit relatives in Tumut. In fact, she was the wife of the station master of Bethungra, a little town midway between Cootamundra and Junee. When the train whistled through the station at Bethungra, this woman's husband became concerned and phoned ahead to the next town, Illabo. Sure enough, the train ran another red light there. By now the stationmasters were becoming very worried.

At Junee, hundreds of people were waiting for the victorious team to return – but the train flew straight through the station, coming to a stop hundreds of yards beyond it. Eventually, the drivers reversed it and we could all disembark.

This story of some happy footballers having a bit of fun still makes me smile, but can you imagine if it happened today!

★

Both Mum and Dad were so proud of all their kids. When I finally broke through and became a commentator, they would tell my story to anyone who had the time and manners to listen.

Mum died in 1983. I wasn't there, but it was Melbourne Cup Day, from memory. Empire Rose, a big mare from New Zealand, won the Cup that year. Mum will always be my Empire Rose, big and beautiful.

Dad and I became much closer after that. As I got older, I started to realise just who this bloke was, and how good he was. On his death bed in 1996, he uttered a simple message to me: 'Give up the gamble.'

What? I thought. *Give up the gamble?*

Dad knew you can't win on the punt, and I think he also realised that he was the one who had started me on the caper. I suppose he was worried that it might one day get the better of me. But what he didn't know, as I never told him, was that if he hadn't done that, I wouldn't have had a dream to chase. I would never have been able to make him and Mum proud in the way that I did.

Well, Dad, I still love the punt, but I don't think it has taken me over just yet. And yes, old mate, it was the launching pad that got me to where I am today.

4

COP DAYS

lthough I knew I wanted to become the next Ken Howard, in the meantime I had to find a way to make a living. So I joined the New South Wales Police Cadets, and eventually became a copper in the ACT. Of all of the jobs I disliked having to do as a copper – which included death knocks and participating in post mortems – the thing I despised the most was locking up SP bookmakers. Some of my best friends were SP bookmakers.

'Do I really have to?' I once asked the sergeant. 'I owe this bloke ten quid.'

The first bookmaker I had to lock up was a lovely bloke named Frank 'Bull' McDonald. I arrested him at the Ainsley Rex in Canberra in 1964. SP bookies were everywhere in those days, and were an intrinsic part of the Australian way of life. They were practically a necessity, since in those days it was illegal to bet anywhere but at the racetrack. My first ever bet had been with an SP.

'How long's this going to take?' asked Frank.

'I've got to get a squad car to come and get us,' I told him.

'Why don't we go in my car?' he suggested.

'We can if you want.'

'I'm working at the racetrack this afternoon,' Frank said as we drove to the police station. 'How long will I be here?'

'I just have to put you through the charge book, take your belt and tie off you, and put you in the cells until you get bailed,' I replied. 'By the way, can I get a lift to the track with you this afternoon?'

And I did. Then the horse I backed with Frank McDonald for ten shillings – Fire Band – won its race! On any other day I would have won £10 off him. Little did Frank know that while he was fielding on the races, the copper who had just arrested him was sitting on the roof of the grandstand, binoculars in hand, practising to become a race caller. Believe me, I felt sorry for Frank McDonald.

If I'm fair dinkum, in all the different jobs I did after leaving school I was simply killing time. For all that time I was hoping and praying that one day I'd get the chance to do what I really wanted to do.

I had left school at 14 and five months, and my first job was as an apprentice fitter. Then came the police cadets, then I went back to the railways as a clerk. It was then that I was transferred to Quirindi, a little town in the upper Hunter Valley, where I was to be the coaching clerk in charge of ticketing and parcels.

You could do the job in about ten minutes a day, I soon found, and the locals quickly convinced me to play footy for the town's team. I was only an average player but a bloke called Jim Cody – a former Magpie – had dropped my name to someone at the club, saying I was coming to town and they should look out for me. At first I said no, but when the club offered me ten quid a game, I changed my mind in about five seconds.

I lived in a boarding house where the landlady was a Mrs Green. She put about two stone on me in a week. Breakfast was the whole shooting gallery, as were lunch and dinner. I had a great time at the footy club and, surprisingly, was actually scoring a few tries.

Then came one of my great disappointments. The scouts from the mighty St George Dragons came to town to watch the Quirindi Grasshoppers play. Apparently they particularly wanted to look at the centre. There were only two of us, so my hopes rose sky-high – until game day. It wasn't me they were watching but David Burns. He was a good bloke but my ego had taken a hit.

I saw him play one day, and thank God he got the job! I would have been busted good and proper in the big league. As a player, I think I was only ever meant for country footy.

Unfortunately, I couldn't complete that season for the Grasshoppers, as I was headed for a bigger challenge. I was getting married, and that was a little more demanding than playing centre for Quirindi or St George.

Still, my brief time in Quirindi was very memorable. This was the area from which the Wynn family originated, and Peter and Graeme – both great players – became fond friends. In later years we often reminisced about the hard-fought games between Quirindi and Werris Creek – and particularly the day the pin-up boy from Werris Creek, Harry Callaghan, put me in hospital for a week or two.

Harry was the 'King of the Creek', I learnt; I was invading his territory, and he obviously didn't like it. The first time we met was also the last: I needed only ten minutes to find my way onto a stretcher and into a St John's ambulance.

★

Back in Sydney, and now married, my dream of becoming a sports commentator seemed farther way than ever. I had taken an audition tape around to a few metropolitan radio stations but had got nowhere. I applied to join the police force in Canberra, and I was accepted. So my new wife, Monica, and I were on our way to the national capital.

We would live in Canberra for nearly three years. Despite the fact that I had topped my squad at the academy in Sydney, I didn't enjoy the work. My heart was still set on becoming a sports commentator. I continued to write letters to all the radio stations I could find, and I hoped that some day my chance would come.

In the autumn of 1966 a telegram came to our house in the Canberra suburb of Ainslie. It was from a man named John Finlayson and it read: 'Please ring me regarding a sports broadcasting job I need filled immediately.' This man Finlayson was the manager of the radio station 2LF in Young.

Nanoseconds later I was on the phone to him, and he

told me he needed someone to call the Maher Cup, country rugby league's biggest competition. He asked me just a couple of questions, including whether I had called rugby league before. I hadn't, but naturally I told him I had. Then he offered me the chance I had been dreaming of.

There was a problem, though: I had a contract with the police force, which meant I had to have a meeting with my superintendent.

Finlayson wanted me there as soon as he could get me, so I went to see Superintendent Bernie Rochford a couple of days later. His first question to me was: 'What is this job? What does a sports commentator do?'

'Well,' I said, 'he describes horseraces, the trots, the dogs, football, cricket . . .'

Superintendent Rochford took a deep breath. 'Well, let me have a look at your history. Theoretically, you're brilliant. Practically, you're hopeless. You're not a good copper.'

Despite my desire to be released, I took exception to this. 'What do you mean?'

'You get called to a car accident, it's a fatal, there's blood and you faint,' the super explained. 'We send you to break the news to the relatives and friends, and you become more emotional than they do.'

'Well, that's true,' I said. 'I don't like the sight of blood. And breaking the news of a death to anybody . . . Nobody would like that, surely.'

'You have to help take the corpse to the morgue and assist the pathologist,' he continued. 'You take the brains and weigh them, and then you take the heart and the lungs and weigh them, too.'

'I was never prepared for any of that,' I told him.

'And after you've gone through the post mortem, you become so attached to the family that you go to the funeral.'

'I'm at funerals all the time.'

'So we take you away from that side of the business and put you on point duty, directing traffic,' the super continued. 'You cause a four-car head-on collision . . . And then there's the SP bookmakers you don't want to lock up.'

This was all true. But I also knew that leaving the police force to join 2LF in Young was going to cost me financially – I'd get about a third less of my weekly wage of about $100.

Even so, I sensed that this career, which I had always wanted, was drawing me towards it. This was my chance.

'I've got to go,' I told him.

And he let me. I was like a player going from one club to another, and let's just say there was no transfer fee.

5

MY FIRST TASTE

Young was good to me. It was there I was given the chance to do what I had always wanted to do. It was from my base at 2LF that I first got to know people from West Wyalong, Harden, Temora, Cootamundra, Grenfell and the like. They embraced me and called me their own.

I loved calling their footy and their trots and gallops and dogs. Nine years after leaving school, I was finally in a job that I really wanted to do. For the first time in my life, I looked forward to going to work. I'd taken a pay cut but I was doing what I enjoyed. *Can you believe that?*

The locals were friendly and made me and my family feel welcome. My eldest son, Mark, was born in Young in 1967. I remember taking Monica to the hospital. A few hours later

I rang to enquire about her progress. Lo and behold, they had no record of her. 'She's not here,' they said.

'But she's got to be there,' I insisted. 'I drove her there myself just three hours ago.'

'Sir, are you sure she is in this hospital? Did you take her to Sacred Heart, the Catholic hospital?'

I had no idea there were two hospitals in Young, and sure enough, Monica was in the other one. *Have another drink, you idiot!* In those days, of course, that was what you did. The father didn't attend the birth. Nowadays you're expected to stay and help. There's no way I could have done that.

On radio, my main job was to call the local rugby league, but that was only one day a week. So they got me to sell advertising and do some on-air work as a disc jockey to fill out my weekly hours. I remember doing one show called *With It on 1340*. I was about as 'with it' as a frog in the desert. The show must have been as interesting as a night in the catacombs.

Selling advertising wasn't difficult. 2LF was popular around Young, Cootamundra, Cowra, Harden, Boorowa and Grenfell. Beyond that, it got harder to sell. I had a sales manager, Jeff Condron, who kept sending me to places to sell advertising where the poor buggers couldn't even hear the stations.

Still, Young was a wonderfully embracing place. Sometimes, when you are in the public eye, it works for you positively. People like to know you, to make friends with you. When you're carting garbage, or picking up papers, or driving a taxi, or selling the tickets on the railway, it can be harder to make friends.

Even these days, I find it wonderful when people approach me and tell me they like my work on air. I soak it up because it makes me realise that I must be giving some people some enjoyment. It wasn't always like that. It took a long time for a lot of people to get to like me.

These days, I'm a little embarrassed by the number of people, particularly kids, who want to have a photograph with me. They probably don't even know my name but they're shaking my hand and high-fiving me. I was in Terrigal, on the NSW Central Coast, recently and I ran into a big bunch of blokes on a buck's party. I must have taken 20 photographs with them.

That sort of thing is easy enough to do. It's much easier than brushing people off. Some of these 'high-brow' people do that. They just brush past people and don't give them the time of day. They must be living on another planet. What you have to do is work out who's fair dinkum and who's not.

When I left the police force and its unpleasantness, I hadn't realised that seeing so much death and assisting the pathologist at autopsies had turned me into a hypochondriac. I was at the doctor's surgery nearly every day. That was the only down side of an otherwise perfect time in my life. I had the job I wanted, and Monica and I had our first child, Mark. Things were good and we had some funny times.

I'll never forget doing the afternoon shift at 2LF one day and going to the toilet for a quick visit. I pulled up my strides, preparing to go back into the studio, and then noticed the toilet was full of blood. I froze. For a 'hypo' like me, the sight of blood is not good. When it's your own, it's terrifying. I went back to the studio and cross-faded the record that was ending into the Beatles' 'Hey Jude'.

'Hey Jude' ran for seven minutes and seven seconds. I ran to the manager's office to tell him of my drama and of my impending death. He didn't believe me. 'I think I'm dying,' I said. 'I'm going to the doctor's – I'm bleeding to death!'

'You can't go now,' he spluttered. 'You're on air!'

But I was already out the back door and across the laneway to the doctor's. The receptionist at the surgery didn't seem concerned. She'd seen me there nearly every day for the past six months.

After waiting for about a minute, I said to the girl, 'Darling, I don't think you understand, but I am sitting here bleeding to death and no one seems to care!'

She scurried down the corridor and returned with the doctor. He was a nice bloke, Alan Oxenham. He took me into the consulting room and told me to jump on the bed. A few seconds later, he said, 'You've knocked the top off a haemorrhoid. You're not bleeding to death. You'll be fine.'

I went back to work and found the manager doing the afternoon show – he was still trying to explain what had happened to the previous announcer. It was bloody embarrassing. 'Hey Jude' had not long finished when I returned to the chair.

Rugby league was big in the Riverina, and the competition everyone wanted to see and hear was the Maher Cup. Fans would charter trains to go and see the games, which were played on Saturday afternoons; the players would back up the next day for their Group Nine competition games.

That's unheard of these days. Saturday arvo footy is taboo, for one thing – and to back up the next day? You've got to be joking. But these blokes did it, and I guess they carried giant-sized hangovers into the Sunday game.

I'd grown up listening to John O'Reilly calling the Maher Cup. I still think he was the best footy caller I've ever heard on radio. He had a silky-smooth voice, and he was incredibly accurate. He went on to become the ABC's top radio caller in Sydney, although that limited the number of people who heard him. I wanted to follow John to the big smoke. I just hoped I'd one day be as good as he was.

The first game of footy I called was in 1966, between Barmedman and West Wyalong. I was so keen that I drove over 100 kilometres of dusty road from Young to Barmedman to watch training on the Tuesday, and I did the same thing on Thursday night at West Wyalong. At the match itself, I was so nervous that I kept a milkshake container of Mylanta with me, taking sips to keep from vomiting.

Calling the footy was fabulous, but it dried up for me when a rebel group called the Murrumbidgee Rugby League broke away from the Maher Cup competition. So I turned to the trots, the dogs and the races. I don't know whether the rebel group buggered things or not by splitting the local community, but they didn't help the Maher Cup, that's for sure.

Making the switch to the trots, gallops and dogs was no

drama. In fact, it set me back on course to do what I had always really wanted to do, but the resident racecaller wasn't impressed. He lost some of his jobs to me, but the reality was that he suddenly had some competition, which he'd never experienced before. For my part, I wasn't about to knock back the opportunity to call whatever was offered.

That is why I will always be indebted to the racing and trotting clubs of Young, Temora and West Wyalong. They made their own decisions without outside influences, allowing me to call races as well as work for 2LF.

So many people and clubs took a gamble on me and stuck with me during the three years I spent at 2LF. It was tough to leave when Garth Carey from 2GB phoned me. I'll always remember Young fondly. It gave me my start, just like it had many others in the industry. As I was leaving, a young blue-eyed bloke called Kenny Sutcliffe arrived. Didn't he kick on?

Anyway, it was Garth who pushed the green light on my career, with one phone call. 'We want you to come to Sydney,' he said. 'You'll be with Ken Howard and John Tapp as their understudy.' Ken wasn't far off retirement, and the station needed a backup who could also call other sports. Garth knew I could do that.

Vince Lombardi, the great American football coach, once said, 'If you shoot for the stars, shoot for the highest one.' That's what I did, in a small way. Ken Howard was the best, and to aspire to emulate anyone else was shooting for a lower star. Whether I reached his heights didn't really matter – I would be setting my ambition high and doing my best. That is all anyone can ask in life.

So, from Junee and the marbles, via Young, the Maher Cup, the police force and a thousand other jobs, and 20 years after having that first bet on a horse called Playboy, the maiden who won the Derby, I moved to Sydney in 1969. It had been a long journey but was well worth the ride.

My old Valiant was chock-a-block. It grunted and groaned but at least it got us to Sydney. We'd only been there five minutes when the chance to buy a house at Seven Hills came up. We paid $11,250 for a three-bedroom redbrick cottage. I didn't have the ten per cent deposit, so I sold the Valiant for exactly the $1125 needed.

6

THAT VOICE

He would walk off the set at Channel Nine on a Saturday morning and head straight to the track. He'd be wearing an off-white suit, a matching hat, a loud tie and beautiful shoes. He'd come into the commentary box, take off his hat and coat and roll a cigarette. When he talked to me he sounded exactly like he did on the air: 'How ya goin', sport?' He was Ken Howard.

His modus operandi on race days was to go to Channel Nine and do a morning racing show with Clarence the Clocker, then he'd come to the track, call the program and head back to Nine to do the nightly news. He'd then go straight home to his wife, whom he affectionately called 'Dicko'. He often talked about having a scotch with Dicko. He never went to pubs or clubs. The only time I ever drank with him was when he'd come into the 2GB studios, which back then were in Phillip Street in the Sydney CBD. Sometimes we'd entice him to play a game of snooker with us at lunchtime at the NSW Leagues Club.

Ken was a shy man, and generous. When he heard I'd moved my family into the house in Seven Hills but had sold the Valiant to do so, he put a handful of notes in my pocket after his horse Liddell – which he had heavily backed – had won. It was about $100, enough to buy me an old utility.

That's as close as I really got to Ken, my boyhood idol. I don't believe anybody ended up too close to him. He didn't give me a hell of a lot of advice, just some tips here and there. He never told me how to call. But he did give me one piece of advice that I've remembered throughout my entire career.

'I don't like these blokes who are bagging people unnecessarily,' he said. 'I've lived by the theory, and I've done okay, that if you've got nothing nice to say about somebody, say nothing at all.'

It was a different time back then, and that was the creed that many callers had. There was more respect. The greats of sports broadcasting, the ones before me, had managed to do it. Young callers today – and I won't name them – are in danger of crossing that line. They can't make themselves older and more mature, but they ought to sound like they are.

If anybody was entitled to be critical of a ride by a jockey, it was Ken. He was the best in the business, but he made it clear to me that I was a whipper-snapper, a wannabe. The listener out there, who was part of the blue-singlet brigade, who might have been part of the needy or the greedy, he was the punter, and he didn't want some snotty-nosed kid telling him that his certainty had been beaten.

You need some whiskers on your face before you can become a controversial commentator. Even today, more than four decades since I started, I prefer to let my co-commentators have the stronger opinion. They're paid to give the expert commentary, while I'm paid to do the play-by-play and to inject some excitement into our telecast. So I don't cross into Peter Sterling's ground, and I don't cross into Phil Gould's ground. They're the experts and I never want to be that person. Even though I've got opinions, I keep them to myself – other than on rules, referees or how I think the game can improve.

John Tapp called races with that attitude. When it came to rugby league, so did a man called Frank Hyde.

Francis Patrick Aloysius Hyde was a centre who played 90 matches for Newtown, Balmain and his beloved North

Sydney during the 1930s and 1940s, but it was his broadcast career for 2SM – which started in 1953 – that made him a rugby league legend. His signature call for a successful shot at goal – 'It's long enough, it's high enough and it's straight between the posts!' – is as much a part of the game's fabric as the goalposts themselves.

He called 33 consecutive Grand Finals, most of them from a card table perched on the sideline of the SCG. In fact, that was the first time I met Frank: at the card table, at the famous ground we all love.

Incredibly, when I first came to Sydney and started on the footy, there were five stations covering rugby league: Hyde was at 2SM, Tiger Black was at 2KY, John O'Reilly was still at the ABC, Col Pearce was at 2UE, and Brian Surtees was at 2GB. Eventually, I took Brian's place simply because I was on the permanent staff and he was a casual. It had nothing to do with his ability – he was a fine caller. Instead of having me get cups of coffee for Ken Howard at the races, 2GB decided to send me to the football on the Saturday, and also on the Sunday.

On this day at the SCG, I was a rookie. I walked out to the card table, and there was Frank Hyde, surveying the scene.

Frank was everyone's friend, and he got away with it.

Today, things are different and it seems you can't do that. There doesn't seem to be any place for the nice guy any longer, and to be frank with you – pardon the pun – I don't like that.

Today, station executives want commentators to be more critical, more controversial, sniping at the opposition, more investigative. Hyde was never like that. He called the game, he promoted the game and I guess he never had any enemies. In fact, when I needed help on a couple of occasions, Frank was the first to put up his hand. That attitude doesn't seem to exist in the Sydney media anymore.

When you called football from the card table, the tricky thing was that you could see some of the players only from the waist up. Such was the rise and fall of the SCG. It was from this perspective that I called my first NSWRL Final: the 1971 decider between South Sydney and St George.

The Rabbitohs had a monster pack, and also featured superstars like John O'Neill, Bob McCarthy, John Sattler, George Piggins and the goalkicking genius fullback Eric Sims. The Dragons had two of the greats: Graeme Langlands and Billy Smith. Souths led 1–0 at half time, before winning

16–6, thanks largely to the work of Piggins at hooker. It remains the last time Souths won the premiership.

In the eyes of many Rabbitohs fans, it was as much a win for me as for them. I've been called 'Rabbits' my whole life, for obvious reasons. But Ken Howard really took to it when I came to Sydney. When a country bumpkin from Young walked into the box one day, he called me 'Rabbit'. Ken heard the comment and carried it on. The South Sydney club and its fans then started to embrace me, thinking that this young caller must follow the Rabbitohs.

So, after Souths won the 1971 Grand Final, I was invited onto the players' bus on the not-so-long trip from Moore Park to the leagues club across the road from Redfern Oval. Everyone was swooning around all these greats, and that night I was christened into the Rabbitohs family – by mistake.

Everyone has known me as 'Rabbits' or 'Rabs' ever since.

★

When I wasn't calling the football or required in the studio, I'd rely on John Tapp for a lift to the races. He was a great mate. He picked me up and dropped me off – I was buggered without him! The ute I'd bought was fine to get me around town, but Tappy and I mainly did the provincial races, as well as the Harold Park trots. He was the number one understudy to Ken Howard, and I was number two.

I was happy with that. To be under Ken and John made me very proud. Ken was one of the greats and Tappy was outstanding. He took me through a tough period, picking me up when I was down, giving me encouragement. He was just about my closest ally and confidant. Unfortunately, when I focused on football later in my career we grew apart, but that happens, doesn't it?

John and I went to the Hawkesbury, Kembla, Gosford and Wyong gallops, among many others, and I'll never forget my first calls at the first two of these.

At Hawkesbury and at Kembla you'd often get a heat shimmer: wave above wave of heat shimmering through the lenses of the binoculars and making it almost impossible to read the colours. For my first calls at both Hawkesbury and Kembla, I had two big fields with a lot of orange colours in them. Let's just say they weren't my best calls. *That's it*, I thought. *I can't do this job.*

Tappy and I had some very funny times. Like the day my old utility met its death 50 yards from Tappy's house, on one of the strangest and funniest nights of my life.

We'd been to Kembla. The jockeys went to the barrier for the first but came back and refused to ride. It was just about the first time they'd ever refused to ride because of the state of the track, so it was a big story. Everyone who had driven down to Kembla from Sydney had nothing to do except go home. Tappy and I were too smart for that, though.

We decided to spend the afternoon at the nearby golf club, playing snooker and getting on the drink. Fortunately, we had a driver with us who didn't drink. Thank goodness he was there, because we really let our hair down. Maybe that's a bit of an exaggeration, since Tappy had very little. I let my hair down a lot.

Tappy was always a bit reluctant to be late home without some excuse. As the night went on, I kept reminding him of the time but he didn't seem too concerned. We must have spent about five hours at the club. As we left, staggering around and looking for the car, I fell in a bloody great ditch full of water and bulrushes.

Tappy finally managed to pull me from the mire, and I emerged looking and smelling like the Loch Ness Monster. We were rolling around with laughter.

'What are you going to tell your missus?' I asked him as we motored home.

'No worries,' he said. 'I've already told her there was a protest on the last so we're running a bit late.'

Poor Johnny must have thought his wife was so stupid that she wouldn't watch the news on TV. The jockeys' strike was the biggest racing story in years, and here he was thinking his wife wouldn't know about it.

'Aren't you worried about getting into trouble?' I asked him.

'You're kidding, aren't you?' said Tappy. 'I'm in charge at my joint.'

'Fine,' I smiled. 'Just asking.'

Our driver dropped us off at my old ute, which I'd parked on a hill around the corner from John's house in Old Toongabbie, because it always had to be clutch-started. We had sobered up considerably during the fairly long drive, and I drove him around to his front door. As we drew up to his driveway, his wife was coming down the front steps. She was white with rage.

'So you've finally arrived,' she said. 'Nice cock and bull story.'

Tappy stuttered and shook and begged me not to leave him as he got out of the passenger-side door. The moment he was out, I dropped the clutch and the accelerator at the same time and was gone in a cloud of blue smoke like I was Alain Prost.

I didn't get far. The last thing I saw was a telegraph pole about a hundred yards down the road. The bonnet ended up on the dashboard, and the car's only hubcap went flying into someone's front lawn.

In time, John and I both went on to the divorce court. It was inevitable, I suppose. Our wives were both good women, the type you would marry. The trouble was that he and I came home too late, too often.

Another time, John and I were under siege from our boss at 2GB. The network stations had been complaining about us turning up late for a preview of that day's racing, which was always supposed to be half an hour before the first race. We received warning after warning.

John had separated from his wife some time before, and was now courting the woman who became his second wife. We had agreed that on Friday nights, when we would broadcast the Harold Park trots to the network, he would do the first half of the program and I'd do the second. The system worked well for two weeks. On the third Friday, I was at a pub near the radio station, having one or two before I went to the trots to take over from John.

It was around 7.25 pm, and the first race was in five minutes. I had a tip in the race so I left the pub and found my way to the control room in the 2GB studio. 'Put me through to Tappy,' I said to the engineer. I wanted to get the tote odds and the bookmaker prices on the nag I was going to back. The engineer looked at me vacantly. 'He's not there,' he said.

I remembered the boss blasting us for being late only three weeks ago. I knew I had to do something, so I told the engineer to let me take control. I had a headset tuned to 2UE and Des Hoysted, and I planned to copy whatever Des said. In other words, I'd listen to 2UE on a trannie, pinch his broadcast and use it from our studios. No one would ever know I wasn't at the track. I had to do it to save both our backsides.

All was going well until halfway through the race, when the engineer began waving his arms about, trying to tell me something. I turned my head towards him in the control room, and suddenly I lost 2UE; the headset was a directional thing, so I couldn't hear Des! Without him I was stuffed.

I lunged for the dial – now I had 2CH, which was playing golden oldies. *I'm about to become a golden oldie myself*, I thought. Now all I could do was call the race from the papers in front of me – but without Des in my ear, how would I know the result?

Turn the mic off, I told myself. *Give yourself some time to think, Rabs.*

The engineer was now able to communicate with me. John was at the track and could hear everything, he said. But I couldn't cross to him without giving myself up.

I found 2UE again as Des finished his call. I wrote down the numbers and then turned my mic back on and apologised to the network for the line dropping out. I gave them the result and the dividends, then announced that John would be calling the second race in 30 minutes' time.

By now the engineer had realised what I'd done. He was frothing at the mouth and said he was going to tell management.

'Go for your life, mate,' I told him. 'Do what you must.'

Next, Tappy was on the phone. 'Mate, what have you done?' he cried.

'I've tried to protect your arse as well as mine!' I said. 'That's what I've tried to do, anyway.'

'Geez, mate,' he said. 'I appreciate that, but shit, I think you've broken the law.'

'John, does it really matter? No one got robbed. I didn't do it for personal gain, I did it to protect us and our jobs.'

'Yeah, I know that,' he said. 'Leave it to me. And Rabs, by the way . . . Thanks.'

He never did tell me where he got to and why he was late. Tappy and I had several drinks with the boss the next night. We all finished pie-eyed but the matter never saw the light of day.

7

TV LAND

Broadcasters rarely receive awards, and that's okay by me. But when I was inducted into the Men of League Hall of Fame in Grand Final week in 2013, it was one of the proudest moments of my career.

There were two reasons. Balmain legend Keith Barnes was also inducted on the same night as I was, and that meant a lot, because he was my first expert commentator when I called rugby league on television.

I was also pleased to join an honour roll that included the late supercoach Jack Gibson and his offsider, Ron Massey. 'And the former great commentator, Frank Hyde,' I told the room. The applause was deafening.

Calling the Amco Cup in 1974 was really the start of my

television career. I'd called the dogs on TV a couple of years earlier, but this was my first big go at the visual medium. Sports promoters Col McLellan and Max Dutch, along with the all-powerful NSW Rugby League boss Kevin Humphries, had a plan to launch a midweek competition. Back in those days, all the clubs in the first-grade premiership were from Sydney. The Amco Cup brought teams together from all over the place: from Queensland and the bush, and even from Papua New Guinea. They asked me to be the commentator.

Straight away, though, I ran into politics. Channel Ten was to carry the product, and they wanted their own personalities to front the thing. Kerry Buckeridge got the job and they asked me to co-commentate. I was totally out of my depth as an expert commentator. People don't want nobodies doing that – they want experts.

'Bucko' did his best. He was a good caller and a good bloke, but then, after about six weeks, he hit a hurdle. Many years later, a pressman accused me of plotting his demise. Nothing could have been further from the truth. The only person who knows I didn't stab Bucko in the back is Bucko, so that's where it lies and forever will.

When I took over, Keith was appointed as my co-commentator, but on one occasion I had Frank Hyde sitting right next me. Frank was a great caller, but he wasn't prepared to help me out on this night at Leichhardt Oval, Balmain's home ground, when we were calling a double-header.

I'd taken on board a fair amount of soft drink when I was calling the first game (these days I live on cups of tea, with a certain amount of water as well), and there was no break between the two fixtures. In the third quarter of the second game, I was busting to use the toilet. I wrote a note to Frank and slid it over to him: 'Could you take over for five minutes? I need to go to the toilet.'

It didn't take long for a response to come: 'No thanks.'

Why would he say no? When I thought about it later, I realised Frank had never called night-time football. Even in those days, he wasn't what you'd call a young man. And Amco Cup matches were tough to call: they could have been between Central Queensland and Western Division, or Port Moresby and Wide Bay.

I was in trouble. The urge was growing, and the pain was becoming excruciating. I grabbed an empty drink bottle and thought to myself, *I'm going to have to do this*. I took the top off the bottle and began to relieve myself.

I continued to call the match as I weed into the bottle. Then I felt a hot sensation down my leg: *I've missed the neck of the bottle!* My only consolation was that my pants were black.

When full time came, the lights went on for me to do an on-camera piece in the broadcasting box. I had a bench in front of me but it didn't matter. With the heat from the lights, it was now very humid in the box and steam was rising from my pants. Embarrassing and uncomfortable, but we plodded on. The show had to come first! Thanks, Frank.

Another night, another Amco Cup double-header, this time at Lang Park in Brisbane. The first game was between two Sydney sides, the second featured Combined Brisbane versus Port Moresby. Game one wasn't difficult because I knew the players from Sydney very well. But I had no way of studying the players in game two.

Normally, I'd go into the sheds and study the faces of players I didn't know. But because this was a double-header, game one finished and game two kicked off immediately.

The Brisbane side was no problem, but the boys from PNG were a nightmare. Needless to say, they were all dark and with fuzzy hair. They had numbers but only on the backs of their jumpers, which made it difficult if they were running at me. So, rather than stutter and stammer my way through the telecast, I took a punt that they wouldn't be scoring too many tries and that the telecast wasn't going back to Port Moresby. I wondered: *What would Ken Howard do?*

You guessed it: don't let the truth get in the way of a good story. Whenever the Port Moresby players had the ball, I looked down at the program and called a name at random. I called whatever name my eye landed on.

Obligingly, they only scored one try, and believe it or not, no one said boo. The final score was 64–4, and the next day one of the execs at Ten said it was one of the best calls he'd ever heard. Poor, simple fool!

There were other matches that also stand out in my memory. In the first year of the Amco Cup, the Cinderella story was the country team from Western Division. It was coached by Johnny King, the former St George winger, and one of their feature players was a bloke who became known as 'TV Ted' Ellery.

He probably was the game's first 'impact player', as we now know it. Because of the larger number of reserves and the four quarters of Amco Cup matches, Ted would be thrown into the game when the coach thought the team needed his fearless, bull-at-a-gate charges through the rucks.

He wasn't the type to give you an 80-minute performance. But he was a real TV star and everybody liked him. He was the image of the old country Aussie battler: raw-boned and with a never-say-die attitude.

Ted and his side were given the home ground advantage for their semi-final against Manly. The venue was set down for Wade Park, Orange. I was given the choice of flying or driving there, so for me the decision was simple: I'd drive up a day early. So I headed up the Bells Line of Road towards the Blue Mountains, through to Lithgow, down the other side to beautiful Bathurst, and then on to picturesque Orange. I checked into the Hotel Canobolas, where the Western Division team was also staying.

Naturally, the officials were at the bar. We had a drink, then some dinner, then another drink. In fact, quite a few drinks. I retired for the night. There had been a nip in the air. It wasn't hard to sleep, but when the phone rang at six the next morning it was hard to wake up.

Col McLellan, the promoter of the Cup, had an unmistakable, deep, booming voice. It would wake the dead. 'How's your weather?' he asked.

'Col, it's six in the morning,' I croaked. 'What's the weather got to do with anything?'

'We're told, here in Sydney, that there's been heavy snow up there. What can you see?'

'At the moment only the bedclothes and the doona,' I replied. 'You've got to be joking. Give me a minute, I'll take a look.'

I thrust back the drapes and there it was – a big chill. There was snow everywhere, and thick. It was an unbelievable white carpet.

'Col, it's true,' I said into the phone. 'It has snowed, and heavy.'

Manly couldn't land in Orange until 3 pm. The game started an hour later, and Western Division won the match on a countback of penalties after it was a draw at full time. It wasn't the best preparation for the Sea Eagles, who'd had to get their gear on while they were still in the plane. At 12-all, Mark Willoughby had missed a kick at goal to win the game. The siren had sounded and Manly were gone.

I had never been so cold. Bill Mordey, a legendary old-school reporter from the *Daily Mirror*, was my co-commentator that day. He followed me up a ladder to the temporary commentary box. It was a scary climb, and we rocked in the wind. He was mumbling and grumbling about the conditions. He refused to work on the Cup ever again. I'd have done the same if I could – the turbulence was frightening.

The after-match scenes were controversial, and anticlimactic in some ways. In a drawn match, the team with the most tries won. If they were level on tries, the team that gave away the fewest penalties won. 'TV Ted' and his gang had beaten Manly. They went on to beat Penrith in the Grand Final to win the inaugural midweek Cup. Cinderella would have been proud.

The Amco Cup was my launching pad into the future. Racecalling was great and I enjoyed it, but I knew where I stood. In 1978, after I'd spent four years working for 2GB and calling the Amco Cup as a freelancer, Ten made me an offer to work for them full-time.

The decision was a tough one but I accepted. I knew I had to be realistic. Football was taking over, and I was getting older. There were two prominent up-and-coming callers: John Tapp behind Ken Howard at 2GB, and Ian Craig behind Des Hoysted at 2UE. I was third in line, at best. Basically, for me to become a leading racecaller, either John or Ian would have to get hit by a bus.

The move to Ten rewarded me in many ways. The first was that it allowed me to realise my long-held dream of calling a Melbourne Cup. That's the dream of every racecaller, of course, just as it is the dream of every trainer and jockey to win it. I called three of them: Belldale Ball in 1980, trained by Colin Hayes and ridden by Johnny Letts; Just A Dash in 1981, trained by Tommy Smith and owned by the property tycoon Lloyd Williams; and Gurner's Lane's miracle win over Kingston Town in 1982. The crowd was numb that day – it was like a funeral.

Working for Ten also allowed me to call first-grade rugby league from 1981, when we won the rights to broadcast the Winfield Cup. I'd called Grand Finals for 2GB, of course, but the early 1980s was a special time: an era of the gold and blue of Parramatta, and the blue and white of Canterbury.

It never ceases to amaze me how people connect me with the Parramatta Eels. In some ways I can understand it, but still I find it hard to fathom.

Since my arrival in Sydney, my base has always been around the Parramatta area: Seven Hills, Northmead and now Castle Hill. I know that an element of the blue and gold rubbed off on me, especially in the early 1980s. I became mates with Ray Higgs, Joe Joseph, Ray Price, Michael Cronin and big

Arthur Beetson. Strangely enough, I never did become too close with Sterlo back then. He was of the younger brigade.

Because of that association, I can understand why some people thought I was a Parra fan, and I'll admit I did get a kick out of seeing them win premierships, which they did in 1981, 1982, 1983 and 1986. But by the late 1980s, my friendship with the club ran aground.

My youngest son, Chris, who was born in 1970, had represented the Eels at S.G. Ball level in 1987, and his side went through unbeaten. He was also in the first Parramatta Marist College side to win the Commonwealth Bank Cup, the pinnacle of schoolboys' rugby league.

When it came time for him to graduate to Jersey Flegg, Chris was told he wasn't required. We don't blame anybody for that. But the kid had given the Eels good service, and if you cut his wrists he'd have bled blue and gold.

Suddenly, Parramatta was looking everywhere for talent, and many of the kids who loved them and would die for them were sent packing. The new recruits didn't have the Parramatta passion. Significantly, an era began in which the great club went downhill. My young bloke went to Wests, as did some of the other rejects. When Parra played Wests I was there leading the cheer squad, barracking for the Magpies.

No hard feelings, but blood is thicker than water and always will be.

When the Eels won the premiership in 1981, it was my first Grand Final on television and the first competition victory for the club. I was at the leagues club that night, and saw the jubilant Parra fans celebrate the breakthrough premiership. The club had tried for so long to win it and had fallen at the final hurdle several times.

I had the honour of being on stage and introducing the premiership players one by one to the adoring crowd. Then came their coach, Jack Gibson, who uttered a line that everyone remembers: 'Ding, dong, the witch is dead!'

It was an amazing night. Little did we realise that there was more of the same to come in quick succession. Ironically, though, Big Jack's words came back to haunt me in 1986, after I'd called the last match ever played by Ray Price and Mick Cronin.

I was about to go into forced retirement, just like Pricey and the Crow.

8

THE CUP

When you start out rolling marbles and calling them as if they were horses, then describing the country's biggest race is always going to be your greatest ambition. And that's the Melbourne Cup, of course. I called three of them – and it was the most stressful thing I've ever done.

The lead-up is intense, and if you're doing it for the first time . . . well, believe me, the intensity is even greater. I started building up my knowledge of the colours weeks before, as some of the Cup entrants ran in other major races. To call races well, you need to be doing it all the time. I was only calling very occasionally because of my decision to take the job at Ten calling the footy.

Even though I was out of practice, Brian Morris, my boss at Ten, knew it was a dream of mine to call the Cup. So when in 1980 he made it possible for me to actually do it, I had to accept the challenge. Funnily enough, I nearly didn't make it to the race.

Weeks in advance of the race, Ten sent me to Flemington to find a suitable broadcasting position. At one stage I found myself creeping around on the roof of the main grandstand, trying to get a look at a spot adjacent to the judge's box. I crawled out onto a beam high above Flemington so I could get a true appreciation of the position and the angle.

Then I thought: *What the hell am I doing out here?*

It was a good question. Suddenly, my total lack of balance and my fear of heights combined, and I fell. I landed on the roof about six feet below – beyond that was a drop of about 100 feet. Thankfully, the roof held my weight, although I left quite a dent in the aluminium. It was as close as you can come to the end, and I can assure you I said a few prayers afterwards.

From the time the Cup field was announced, late on the Saturday of Derby Day, I would start studying the final colours for the horses that would race on the first Tuesday in November. I studied hard, particularly the similar sets of colours. If the jockeys' silks were almost the same, I'd take the colour of the horse into account too. I'd factor in the riding style of the jockeys, the colour of the livery, any conspicuous markings each horse carried. All that might seem unimportant, but let me tell you, it could be vital.

In the 1979 Cup, the stablemates Salamander and Love Bandit both carried blue and white stripes. They put a red cap on one rider, a white cap on the other. A few hundred yards out from the start, one of the caps blew off. Callers and spectators were left watching a horse in blue and white stripes with no cap, and it was involved in a very close finish – but was it Salamander or Love Bandit?

Such was the case with my first Cup call the following year. Master trainer Colin Hayes had two runners, both owned by the late British billionaire Robert Sangster: Bohemian Grove and Belldale Ball. They had the same owners' colours, so jockey John Letts, who rode the winner, Belldale Ball, wore a red cap.

Calling the Melbourne Cup – or any race, for that matter – is a lonely and nerve-racking experience. You can't say, 'Stop the race, I've forgotten a set of colours!' Still, it's wonderfully satisfying when the race is over. There really is no other singular sporting event that captures the *entire* nation.

But it's a real challenge for racecallers – the ultimate test. I didn't like reading the sports news, because there was no challenge. When you are calling the Cup, you're on your own. There's no mechanical device to help you. If you're in trouble, the only thing you have to help you is your own ability. There is no autocue. That's why it is our Everest.

When I called my second Cup, in 1981, Just A Dash won; the legendary Tommy Smith was the trainer. He'd won the race only once before, with Toparoa in 1955, beating the champion gelding Rising Fast. Peter Cook was the jockey. The aftermath of that Cup, with scenes of tears and high emotion, were overwhelming.

Pete's father, Bill, was a champion jockey in his own right, but he wasn't well. Pete knew that and made one of the most sincere and emotional speeches I've heard at a Melbourne Cup presentation. He was one of the most gifted jockeys I've ever watched. He was just so talented. He had hands of silk and the patience of Job.

His father was obviously a great mentor, and Peter learnt quickly. In 1991, though, he suffered permanent heart damage following an incident while using a sauna in the jockeys' room at Canberra Racecourse, and he retired a few years later. It was extremely unfortunate, because I have no doubts he was headed for the absolute top. They talk about the likes of Damien Oliver and Jim Cassidy and Shane Dye; let me tell you, Peter Cook was as good as any of them.

★

My third Cup was in 1982, and it was one of the most memorable in the history of the race. It was the day the great Kingston Town – also prepared by Tommy Smith – failed by only a short margin behind Gurner's Lane.

'Miracle' Malcolm Johnston had the ride on 'the King'. For days leading up to the race they were saying the great horse might not run. He had an injury that was very worrying. In the end, the big black horse did run, and in my opinion he ran the race of his life.

For years afterwards, Johnston had to wear criticism for his ride. I know 'Miracle'. He's explained to me what happened that day, and I believe him. He maintains that with the huge weight the King was carrying – 60 kilograms – it was better for him to come off the fence at around the 800-metre mark, so as to give himself some room to wind the big fella up. As it turned out, this gave a saloon run to Mick Dittman on Gurner's Lane, and Mick improved his position into a winning one.

I remember, as a commentator, willing the King to lift and win, just as the rest of Australia was, but it wasn't to be. 'Kingston's in front, but Gurner's Lane is going to him! Gurner's Lane after Kingston Town. And Gurner's Lane beats Kingston Town . . .'

Kingston Town, one of the greatest ever, had to be content with second, and the fickle and the uninformed alike all bagged Malcolm. He didn't deserve that. He'd taken a punt to win the race, and it hadn't paid off.

At the end of it all, I can only tell you that calling Melbourne Cups was a great and rewarding experience, but for me it was made so damn difficult by the fact that I wasn't 'match-fit', so to speak. I was trying my best to do the biggest job in my world off little preparation. Don't get me wrong, we got there, but I know it could have been much, much better. I had rarely been to Flemington, wasn't calling much racing in those days and hadn't seen the runners as a caller before the big race. That's tough.

We at Channel Ten were reliant on our Melbourne colleagues to make things as simple as possible – technically, strategically and practically. I must admit, I thought that, deep down, some of them were peeved that Sydney had sent down their own caller to do the Cup. I understood then, and I still do, that the Melbourne Cup was a Melbourne thing, but it was also an Australian event. Sometimes it seemed like they wanted the whole thing for themselves.

One night after the Cup, I got on the turps with one of my idols, Bert Bryant. What a caller he was. He could make you laugh even if you had backed a loser. He was easily the most entertaining racecaller I have heard. He knew better than anyone that commercial radio is all about entertainment, and he did that so well. Bert always hosted the Gold Whip function at the Southern Cross Hotel after the race. It was a tradition.

On this particular night we were still in the Flemington car park several hours after the last race. By the time we got to the function, we were three parts tipsy. He still managed to host the function. How? I will never know.

Bert always had plenty of guests around him, and we all retired to his suite. More drinks, and by then some of us were really gone. I vaguely remember taking my last sip as I slid down the wall I was leaning against. I resembled a squashed grape, slowly sliding down the wall, until I finished lying comfortably on the floor on my back.

I can still hear Bertie saying to some waiter, who had arrived with another drink for me, 'Well, don't waste it, just pour it over him.' From that experience I learnt never again to get involved in a drinking session with Bert.

As it happened, we did have one last drink, shortly before he died. A simple whiskey and a laugh, but deep down we knew it would be our last. He was riddled with the dreaded cancer, and it was apparent that the end was nigh.

In my mind, Bert will always be one of the true greats of the track. He understood that the majority of spectators want to be entertained, not lectured. No one did that like Bert Bryant. I loved him.

9

FLYING

There are many ways to tell this story, but we might as well start in the Qantas Club at Sydney Airport. That's where Phil Gould started writing a story that ended up all over the *Sydney Morning Herald* the very next day.

It was Mother Day in 2013, and Gus and I were sitting in the lounge, waiting to board a plane to the Gold Coast that had been significantly delayed because of heavy fog. We were supposed to be calling the Titans–Dragons game from 3 pm, and it was already 12.50 pm. We were no chance. Well, in my mind we were no chance.

I felt we were better off getting Peter Sterling and Tim Gilbert to be on standby at Nine's studios in Willoughby, so they could call it off the television. But Gus had other ideas.

'They're calling us to the gate now,' he said.

Throughout this whole time, while I was concerned about who would call the Sunday football that afternoon, Gus was typing away on his iPad. As I pranced and danced and roved and wandered around, he just watched me and kept typing.

There's an emergency here, I was thinking, *and this silly bastard is sitting there typing a story about something that has no relevance to what we're doing.* Even when we got on the plane, he was laughing and giggling and his big stomach was bouncing up and down. *What the hell is he laughing at?*

I can tell you, I wasn't laughing when we were halfway to the Gold Coast and one of the stewards approached us. 'Mr Warren,' she said, 'when you come off the plane, there will be a car waiting, and they will be taking you to the helipad.'

'The helipad?' I said, incredulously. 'No, we're getting a hire car to the ground.'

'Channel Nine has arranged a helicopter for you,' she informed me.

'A helicopter!' I shouted. 'Are you crazy? I'm not getting into a helicopter!'

'We'll be right, mate,' Gus chimed in. 'Those things hardly ever come down.'

'Shut up, you idiot,' I snapped back.

At 2.42 pm we landed at Coolangatta, then a car took us from the foot of the plane's stairway to the helipad.

'How often do these things crash?' I asked the helicopter pilot after we had scrambled inside.

'Only once,' he grinned.

Gus had insisted that I sat up the front, in the bubble, looking down at the world below us. He sat in the back, still typing away. I was looking at my genitals.

We finally arrived at Robina for the match. As we came out of the lift on the floor where the commentary box was located, with the entire stadium and the Titans and Dragons players waiting for us to arrive, Gus shoved his iPad under my nose. 'Have a read of this,' he said.

'Have a read of what?' I asked, stunned. 'We've held the match up already – we have to report in for duty!'

'Read this,' he said. Gus never listens to what I say.

So I started reading his story, and eventually I started laughing. Then he was hugging me and laughing with me. His story, which he'd filed for the *Herald* the next day, started like this:

I'm sitting in the Qantas lounge at Sydney Airport.
It's 12.34 pm. Our plane to the Gold Coast for

Sunday afternoon football was to leave at midday, but due to a backlog of flights created by a thick fog over Sydney this morning, our flight has been delayed. They said 12.50 pm. Now they're saying 1.15 pm. However, there are no guarantees. Even though the game starts at 3 pm at Skilled Park, Robina, and our chances of actually getting to the ground in time for kickoff are remote, I'm not panicking. You see, I am with the great Ray Warren, and 'Rabbits' has it all under control. I love Rabbits. He is working the phones, feverishly looking for a solution to our little dilemma. I have complete confidence in 'my man'. At this point I can read him like a book.

He was right: he can read me like a book. But I wasn't concerned about getting to Robina, I was more concerned about avoiding the flight altogether. When we walked into the box, we were laughing our tits off. The producer was not impressed. 'What the hell are you laughing about?' he said. 'We've delayed the kickoff and you're laughing?'

★

Where does this phobia of flying come from? Where all my phobias came from: my parents.

I was the son of a railway fettler, and Dad and Mum never boarded a plane in their lives. Planes would go over Junee on their way to Sydney or Melbourne, and they'd always remark, 'If we were meant to fly, we'd have wings.' Funnily enough, the railways' slogan was: 'The railway is the safe way.' They had me brainwashed from the time I was a little kid. I'm not critical of them – it's just who they were. But this did teach me one thing: you shouldn't talk about your phobias in front of your kids, because some of them will rub off.

Mum was very superstitious. If a knife was dropped in our house, the person who dropped it could never pick it up. It had to be picked up by somebody else. That was a phobia: bad luck. It was a curse. She had a mile of them. Don't put your T-shirt on back-to-front or inside-out. If you did, you had to count to ten before you took it off.

I recall my first flight, a trip from Sydney to Moree. I got there in one piece but decided to catch the train back home. Hobart was another of my early aerial excursions. I caught the train to Melbourne, loaded myself with a couple of brandies before the flight, popped a pill under my tongue and wobbled off at the other end, 'three parts elephants'.

Another time, during an airline strike, I was told we were chartering a DC-3 so we could cover a match in Brisbane. The last DC-3 I'd seen was full of bullet holes. I decided I had to get out of this trip, whatever the cost, and in doing so I learnt a valuable lesson.

I told the boss I couldn't go because my dad had taken ill. As it happened, although Dad didn't have many healthy periods in his twilight years, just then he was in peak condition. I didn't go to Brisbane and, sure enough, Dad got very sick the next day and wasn't expected to live.

On another occasion, some press guys I knew had a major scare flying out of Brisbane after an engine blew up; it had been touch and go. Their plane had been a Boeing 727 – one of those things with three engines on its tail. My next trip was one week later, and the incident was playing on my mind.

I got to the airport with no luggage, just a suit carrier. The flight was leaving from Gate 13. I called on all my bravado and got to the gate lounge to look out at the plane, which is something I always do. Sure enough, it was a 727. Leaving from Gate 13! *You're kidding*, I thought. I immediately booked myself onto another flight and headed for the bar to kill a couple of hours and write out an updated will.

Handwritten wills: I've done more than the average

solicitor. In fact, I've written more wills than Robbie Waterhouse has written betting tickets. Just about every time I fly I write a new one. One time I sent an envelope to a friend with a last will and testament inside. On the outside I'd written: 'Not to be opened unless the sender is killed in an accident.' But the recipient didn't read the small print, opened the envelope and rang my missus to express his deepest condolences.

The great John Sattler edged me onto a flight to New Zealand one time with the Australian team. He knew I hated the damn things. When we boarded, he was sitting right behind me. In those days, I always kept the pillows ready by my side, in case of emergency.

We took off, and just as the wheels left the ground and that bloody undercarriage ground up into the bowels of the plane, Satts let go with a full-blooded knee to the back of my seat. I was propelled forward like a rag doll, screaming out that we'd hit something. Needless to say, Sattler and the rest of the Aussie team thought it very funny. The rest of the passengers and crew just looked at me like the aeronautical failure that I was.

I don't know what it is. I fly more than most people. It could simply be an extension of my fear of heights. I always request a room on a lower floor when I stay at a hotel. On a plane, I always ask for a window seat, towards the front, if possible. If I was scared of flying itself, then why would I like to sit by the window and look out? I don't know the answer to that.

Since September 11 happened, things haven't improved. I hate flying in the morning, because if you ask for a drink you look like an alcoholic. They don't serve alcohol in most lounges until after midday, anyway.

Those who say they like flying bemuse me. I reckon they must either be crazy or just be playing at bravery. I'd love to see them in a real emergency. I bet you they'd be the first to start crying for help.

Is it any wonder people get scared on airplanes? You get on board and sit down, and the crew immediately runs through all the safety equipment and the appropriate action you should take in case of emergency. *This is the seatbelt – it must be worn at all times, during take-off, landing and in flight, in case of unexpected turbulence . . .* What does that mean, exactly? We're suddenly going to start bouncing through the sky?

Under the seat you will find your lifejacket. In the event that we land in water, only half-inflate the jacket before leaving the plane. Fully inflate only when outside the aircraft. The jacket is fitted with a light and a whistle. In the unlikely event of an emergency, your hostess will be there to help . . . Good God! She is four-foot-two and 42 kilograms!

So there we are, floating around in the ocean in the pitch black, with a light the size of your thumb and a whistle that will supposedly attract the attention of some unsuspecting fisherman who just might be drifting past in the middle of the Pacific. At least with the light we can continue to read the form guide for tomorrow's races, but from the way they talk, we won't be there in time for the first.

Seriously, all those safety instructions don't really put you in a very relaxed frame of mind.

Finally, they say: 'Now, sit back, relax and enjoy the flight.' What bloody hypocrisy! By now, all I want to do is get off the flight or get a stiff drink. Of course, I can't do either, so I just sit there and freeze, with white knuckles, clammy hands, the whole bit. But I learned long ago that if I wanted to do what I do for a living, then I had to grin and bear it.

★

It's only now, decades later, that I fully understand and can talk about how my fear of flying led to my dismissal from Channel Ten, which set me on a tough path through my life and career for the next five or six years.

Some people believe I was knifed in the back. I've got no proof of that, though. Looking back, I'm certain I was the victim of a well-planned removal in 1986. But with time comes a chance to think rationally, and I've thought about this particular episode in my life quite a lot.

In 1984 I was selected to head Channel Ten's Olympic broadcast from Los Angeles. I was to do the prime-time presentation, and my on-camera co-hosts would be the tennis legend John Newcombe and the Melbourne newsreader Charles Slade.

I was always a fairly nervous bloke, and a certain remark from someone in Ten's management didn't help my state of mind. 'If we stuff these games up,' he said to me, 'it'll be your fault.'

'What do you mean by that?' I asked.

'Well, there are 32 sports, and you're the presenter. You've got to know all there is to know about them.'

I went away and I learnt just about everything there was to know about those 32 Olympic sports. I knew a bit about the obvious ones, but nothing much about the likes of fencing or archery. But I did hours of research, and soon enough I was ready for it. But before I could do the job I had to get to Los Angeles – and that meant a long flight.

The tension in me built up, and in the end I caved in to my fear of flying. I walked into the office of George Brown, Ten's chief executive, a month before the games were due to begin. 'Mate, I've got something to tell you,' I said. 'I can't go.'

'What?' George was stunned.

'I can't go.'

'Well, why not?'

'There's a lot of responsibility on my shoulders – and I'm really scared of flying. I just can't do it.'

He wasn't happy. Ten wasn't happy at all. It was the worst career move I ever made. No one said my decision would come back to haunt me, but I'm sure it played a part in my demise when the vultures started circling. Not going to Los Angeles in 1984 left me vulnerable to those who wanted to see me gone two years later.

I had some wonderful experiences at Channel Ten. For me, the three Melbourne Cups I called in the early 1980s were the clear highlight of my thirteen years there. Ten also gave me my big break into TV, but for all that, my time at the network ended in sad circumstances.

When I think about it, I probably got what I deserved. How could a network employ a guy in this job if he didn't want to fly? In the end, the episode made me appreciate this career of mine, this dream, even more.

When I finally got my second chance – I call it the second draw – I think I was a much better person for it. Being sacked was the biggest learning experience of my life. And when Channel Nine asked me if I was prepared to travel as the job demanded, I told them: 'Yes – even if I have to fly in a gyrocopter!'

10

THE WILDERNESS

Getting the flick from Ten was probably the smack in the face I needed. Just prior to that, my marriage to Monica, which had lasted 22 years, had also come to an end. She was the only girlfriend I ever had, really.

I couldn't blame anyone except myself for the break-up. I had become obsessed with other interests. My priorities were out of whack. Monica was a great mother and still is. When I think back, though, we first met when I was 18 and in the police cadets in Sydney. That was crazy, really, because I never had any desire to be a cop. Monica and I got engaged and then married in 1964. I was 21 she was 20. It's clear to me now that, when we married, Monica was getting a policeman who really wanted to be a sports caller.

After just two years of marriage, I was given the chance to do what I really wanted, and so the cop became a disc jockey and sports caller. Suddenly, I was swept away by the excitement of it all and put all my energy into my work. In the meantime, in many ways I took my eye off the ball at home.

In the end, family is much more important than work, but I had it around the wrong way, big-time. In saying that, had I not put so much energy into my work, perhaps I wouldn't have achieved what I set out to do. Who knows?

I can assure you of one thing: if you are planning to get married and have a family at a young age, and you have a desire to get into radio and TV, think twice. Working in the media is fantastic, but in my case it wasn't compatible with marriage and all the responsibilities that come with it.

That doesn't mean all the marriages of people in my business break up, but believe me, the lifestyle can overpower you. You can lose sight of the really important things in life. You can get immersed in the plastic or make-believe life that you *think* you are in. That in itself is hard to handle.

Adding to the pain of my marriage break-up came a $30,000 bill from the taxation department. I was the innocent victim of some misguided accountancy advice, whereby I was told to form a company and pay company tax rather than remain a normal 'pay as you go' employee. Three years went by, and then *wham*: the ATO said I was not entitled to be a company and therefore owed $30,000.

And at that point I bombed out of Channel Ten. That blow was the hardest of all to cop. It was the way it was delivered. One of my best mates, John Davies, was second-in-charge at Ten, and he asked to be given the task of telling me it was over. It was brave of him, but the way he put it left me wondering what the reason was.

'We've just renewed our contract with the league for the Winfield Cup for another three years,' he told me. 'But you won't be doing it. The network wants Mossop. Even though we think you're the best, they want him.'

Wow, as Gus would say. *Get that into ya.*

I was numb. Although I was confused by logic of the decision, it was quite evident that my time at Ten was coming to an end. I worked at Ten for three months and finished up after the 1986 Grand Final. Life would go on, I realised, so there was no use in me crying about it.

I went back to calling races on the radio more frequently – and probably half-heartedly, I might add. There was no future in that, as I saw it. John Tapp and Ian Craig were both slightly older than me, and both were very good at their jobs. If I was ever to get one of their jobs, by then I'd be on the doorstep of retirement anyway. Without rugby league, I was stuffed.

I drove many miles calling country races – you name the town, I was there. Sky Channel kindly gave me a job compering the dogs on Thursday nights. I absolutely hated it but had to do it. Anything to make ends meet.

In that black period I was trying to get work anywhere, and someone suggested politics. Lo and behold, the Liberals thought that idea had some value. Nick Greiner was premier, so out of the blue he and his wife, Kathryn, came to visit us at our little three-bedroom redbrick home at Northmead. The party wanted me to stand for the seat of Parramatta.

It was nerve-racking having the premier come to our house, but we put on the scones and cream thing. It was a Saturday, however, and that meant it was a major raceday – I had to excuse myself several times, on the pretence that I had to go to the loo, so that I could listen to the neddies.

I will admit that the thought of entering parliament did hold some appeal for me – until the moment Nick told me what I would have to do and what I'd be earning if I was successful. That changed my feelings pretty quickly. The wage as a junior politician was ridiculously low, and I still was holding on to my dream of getting back to calling the sports rather than the numbers.

The silly thing about being well known and in the public eye is that it can work against you just as much as it can work for you. I applied for jobs picking up the garbage and delivering orange juice, but they didn't seem to take me seriously. The bloke with the garbage run laughed his head off.

In 1987 a young bloke almost burnt my house down. It happened like this.

Parramatta Marist Brothers had long been overlooked as a school for young talented kids from the country who were good at rugby league. Both the Parramatta and Canterbury clubs had been putting these kids into Fairfield Patrician Brothers. I made it clear to Denis Fitzgerald, the boss at Parra, that my sons' school, Parramatta Marist, would love to be considered too.

Denis made it happen, and suddenly we were hosting a kid from Nelson Bay.

By this time, I had met my second wife, Cher. We married in 1994 and have been together 29 years now. Cher came to Australia from Wales in 1971 with her parents, Alan and Eve, and her two brothers, Christopher and Julian.

One day Brother Coman from the school rang. 'We

have been given a sponsored kid from the country,' he said. 'He's not Catholic but that doesn't matter – but we can't find accommodation for him.'

So Cher and I took the boarder from the country in to stay for a week while the school found a permanent home for him. He ended up staying with us for about four months, while he helped the school try to win the premier schoolboys' cup.

One weekend Cher and I had to go down to Junee. Mum was not well – she wasn't expected to live, in fact. While we were away, the young footballer put some sausages on the grill, and he also had the deep-fry heating up. Then he decided to go up to the nearby shops in Northmead to get a pizza. On his return, the house was on fire and surrounded by five fire engines.

I haven't seen the kid since. No apology. No 'thanks for having me'. Nothing. I might add, though, that we did win the schoolboys' cup, and he played a major part in that.

Along with the late Brother Coman and David Dwyer, I had a lot to do with the formation of that side. The memories I have of that time are great. Together we encouraged the school to adopt rugby league much more than it had in the past. Coman was a great man, and Dwyer went on to become one of the biggest bookmakers in the country. What happened to the footballer? I don't know. The insurance company paid for the damage to the house, thankfully.

Then, in 1988, my mum died. I've said it before, I know, but she was the best mum in the world. What she had done for me was incredible. I think of Mum and Dad every day. I still love them to bits, and one of my great regrets is that I didn't tell them that every day. When I visit their graves these days, I say a prayer and say how sorry I am about that. Let me tell you this: if you have the chance, tell your mum and your dad every day that you love them.

So, from around 1984 to 1990, my life was depressing in many ways. My marriage ended, my mum died, I was hit with a tax bill, my house half-burnt down, and I lost my job and my dream. The only upside in that time was meeting Cher. Though I wonder: did she know what she was getting involved in?

Seriously, though, I now look back at this time and understand that it helped me see things more clearly. That's why I was able to come through it. From 1990 onwards, I think I have been a much better human being for the experience.

★

After my years in the wilderness, I spent some time on the Sydney radio airwaves at 2KY. I followed the former referee Greg 'Hollywood' Hartley and the former Manly forward Peter 'Zorba' Peters to the station in early 1990s.

I tried my hand at the morning shift, from 9 am to noon, which was a slot once occupied by such icons as John Singleton, Ron Casey and Ita Buttrose. I was the last one to do the morning show before the station was dedicated to racing.

My time at 2KY was a mixed bag. First, I had trouble adjusting to the pro-Labor beliefs that existed there, because in those days the Labor Council of New South Wales owned the station. I was hosting a morning program, and had to do things their way or not at all. I had several run-ins with management, who always seemed to have close ties to the Labor Party. I wasn't going to go that easily to that side of politics. I interviewed a few Liberal candidates on-air, which wasn't received all that brilliantly.

I haven't been politically minded all of my life, but this experience made me lean towards the right side of politics. That said, the people I worked with were the salt of the earth – the engineers, the producer, Steve Hurson, along with Tanya Bracey and Marilyn Carragher. Marilyn read out the day's scratchings at 10.30 am, which took a full fifteen minutes!

The best thing I did at 2KY was enlist my GP and good friend Dr Graham Malouf to come on the morning program and take calls from people on matters of health. He'd spent years treating my illnesses, real and imaginary, so he knew I was a hypochondriac. That added to the fun of the program.

I will never forget the day when one bloke called about his gout.

'Well, mate, you take some Colgout,' I said. 'That will clean you out. And then you take Progout tablets. One per day for the rest of your life.'

'I didn't really want your advice,' the bloke said. 'What's the doc think?'

'Though it hurts me to say it,' Malouf said, 'he's bloody right.'

I gave 2KY away eventually because I was trying to broadcast races from Gosford, and leaving the line open to do drive-time as well. Thankfully, 2GB picked up Doc Malouf, who is still dispensing his advice on a weekly basis.

★

No longer calling the rugby league made it tough for me to go to the football. Truth be told, I was embarrassed. One night, though, somebody convinced me to go a game at Parramatta Stadium. And that was when I had one infamous incident with a newspaperman.

As I walked past his desk in the press area, he referred to me as 'Rabbits'. Then I referred to him by his nickname, which he didn't particularly like. He blew right up! 'You're no good,' he said. 'You're a low, filthy thing. You've been sacked from any job you've ever had.'

That really hurt me because it was bullshit. I'd never been sacked in my life. And even though I sometimes say I got the flick from Channel Ten, technically that was not the case. As I've explained, they did offer me the job of being their racing expert, which was a cop-out, of course, as they had no racing!

So I lost my cool. I went for his jugular. He was on the telephone, and I grabbed the cord and wrapped it around his neck. I was ahead on points, but then I was caught in a full nelson wrestling hold from behind. It was Zorba. He'd come out of the commentary box because we were making too much noise. We'd also knocked over a monitor.

I was later told that when the journo went into the office on Monday, all the telephones were suspended from the ceiling, with the cords dangling down.

I can laugh about it now. I hope the journo can too. I haven't mentioned his name but we've made our peace.

★

Calling an eight-race meeting at Dubbo would earn me no more than $200. I'd have to drive five hours to get there but I really needed the money. And anyway, I loved working in the country. I had made friends and connections in Coffs Harbour and Orange in the past, and the chance to go back and work for a country club was appealing.

Cher and her mother came with me to Dubbo on one occasion. I thought the company would help pass the time during the long drive. Let's just say it was a soothing relief when we got to Dubbo and I could put the headphones on! The sound of the races and trots booming in from all over the country was a welcome change. At least I had control of the volume and I could turn it down!

I'm kidding. Cher and her mother, Eve, are both great women. The ma-in-law is a good stick: she loves a punt and a drink and a chat. And God, doesn't she like a chat . . .

Anyway, there we were at the Dubbo races. The punt was going no good. There was one race left and my wallet was empty. A trainer up in that area was Gary Cooper: a good horseman who had an excellent strike rate. When he produced one, you would normally collect.

Why is it when you've no money left that you always come across the best tip you are ever going to get?

Gary was a dry man and spoke with a quiet country drawl. Seldom did he offer a tip. Seldom did he talk, in fact. He strolled up to me in the saddling yard as the jockeys were being legged up for the last. 'This will win,' he said, and walked away.

Obviously, he meant his own horse, which was fetching the odds of 5 to 2 with the bookmakers. Now, what would you do? Let it run around without getting on it? Bet on the nod? Or ask the club secretary for your wages before the last race?

I beat a path to the secretary's office and asked for early payment. He obliged. With $200 worth of crisp notes in my hand, I charged into the ring. Cooper's horse was now showing 2 to 1.

'Mate, $400 to $200,' I said to Peter Capelin, one of the smiling assassins known as bookmakers.

'For you, I'll make it $500 to $200,' Peter said.

Lovely, I thought. *The fool has bet me overs and Cooper has declared.*

I quickly studied the colours. Cher and Eve came up to the broadcasting box with me, chatting about what they'd put their $2 each-way bets on. I took no notice. Cooper's horse looked beautiful: that was all I was concerned with. They went into the gates, then I started the broadcast, both on the course and on the radio.

At the final turn, Cooper's horse shot clear and I could smell the money. With a hundred yards to go, I was in front – but there was a problem. A jockey wearing a red jacket with a yellow Chinese dragon emblem on his back was flying. The horse's name was Duckbo, and he was owned by a man called Wong who also owned the local Chinese restaurant.

Right on the post, bloody Duckbo grabbed my horse and beat him by a nose. I retained my composure as best I could. *I've done my wages,* I was thinking. *I've got a useless betting ticket, and there's very little petrol in the car for the trip home.*

I finished the broadcast and turned to look at my wife. Somehow, I had to explain why we had no money in the kick and that we needed petrol. I nearly choked on the words, but she continued smiling. If only she knew how much it was hurting me – the pain of getting beaten by a 66-to-1 nag.

'Not to worry, love,' she said, producing a tote ticket for $2 each way on Duckbo.

'Isn't it wonderful?' said the ma-in-law, who had backed Duckbo too.

'Yeah, bloody marvellous,' I muttered. 'Let's go and collect and then find a service station.'

★

As you can tell, Eve didn't mind a punt. One Saturday when she was staying with us, Cher took her down to the TAB to place her bets on her favourite jockey, a bloke called Jamie Innes. It didn't matter what he rode, she was on it. In those days, he barely rode a winner on the city tracks.

I'd told my broadcasting colleague Ian Craig about this mother-in-law of mine, who would back Jamie Innes every time he saddled up. Jamie is a handy jockey but how anyone could religiously follow him was beyond me.

On this particular Saturday, I stabbed the first leg of the daily double at big odds, and I had it going for plenty if the second leg got home. Before race time, I put a little on whatever else in the race seemed to have a chance. In other words, I'd nearly covered the field. My returns were going to be huge. It didn't really matter what came in, except for a couple that had no hope.

So I was outside, washing the car, singing, whistling. It was a beautiful day and the second leg of the double seemed certain to make it even better. The ma-in-law wandered out the front to have a smoke; she also knew I was listening to the races on the car radio, of course.

'They're off!' declared Ian Craig.

My horses were doing well inside the 200 metres. They were running first, second and third, and my worst result was around $2000. It was bloody wonderful! All of a sudden, though, things changed.

'Hello, what's this down the outside?' asked Ian Craig in the call.

Sure enough, it was one of the two horses I hadn't covered. I was gone.

Then Eve pipes up, between puffs on her smoke. 'I wonder what it will pay? I've had two bucks each way. Jamie rode it, you know?'

I felt like putting the hose on her rather than the car.

'So that's $25 the win, and $6 the place,' said Ian Craig – but he didn't stop there. He had to twist the knife a little. 'Wonderful for Jamie Innes, one of racing's battlers, and wonderful for Ray Warren's mother-in-law, Eve. She always backs Jamie, no matter what he is on. Good luck to you, Eve.'

'Did you have something in the race?' she asked me politely.

'No!' Silently, I was thinking more evil things.

I'd love to tell you that this was the only hard-luck story I ever had on the punt. But it's only the beginning . . .

11

THE EVIL PUNT

Gambling has always been a part of my life. These days, I restrict it to horseracing. All the other forms of betting don't get me anymore. That wasn't always the case, mind you: I used to bet on trots, dogs, pokies, cards, flies crawling up the wall – any bloody thing.

On that fateful Saturday afternoon in 1949, when Dad let me have a bet on Playboy, I figured the punt and I were meant to be. If that horse didn't win, I don't believe Dad would've been prepared to stake my little gambles for any great length of time.

As I mentioned earlier, on his deathbed Dad muttered to me to give up the gamble. Coming from him, this seemed a contradiction, but in reality he knew that if he had not let me have that first bet, I probably would never have heard of Ken Howard, never have become fascinated by him and obsessed with being like him, and more importantly never experienced the thrill of living out this unbelievable dream. Now, on reflection, I give thanks to Dad for letting me have that bet, which set me off on this enjoyable journey.

Yes, the gamble has cost me heaps of money. But let me make it clear: I don't recall anyone being deprived of anything as a result of my interests. That's of paramount importance, as is the fact that I only used my own money, unlike those poor buggers who have to steal or beg or borrow to have a bet. They are the ones who are our problem gamblers, and they need help. For them, it is a sickness.

Making that point reminds me why I was disappointed with an article about me back in 2010. The Sunday newspaper in question had asked me to comment on the broadcast of live odds and betting in Nine's telecast of rugby league matches. While talking to the journo, I made the point that problem gamblers will always find a way to bet, no matter what, and I then compared them with people like me. I told the reporter my story to explain myself more fully. Suddenly, he turned the story into one about my supposed problems rather than what he had actually come to talk to me about.

Ray Warren was only six when his father let him
bet sixpence on a horse in the 1949 AJC Derby.
Unfortunately, Warren says, 'the bloody thing won –
and my father gave me the winnings'.

It was the embryo of a 60-year link to gambling
which, Warren admits, cost him the financial
prosperity many expect the master rugby league
commentator would enjoy after 44 years in
broadcasting . . .

'When I think about the money I spent, it
crosses my mind that I could now be living on the
shores of Sydney Harbour,' Warren said.

As I said, the story was never meant to be about me, but that
was the way it turned out. My throwaway line about living
on the harbour was taken out of context. I was talking to
the reporter like two blokes do over a beer at the local club.
All I was trying to do was explain the difference between
problem gamblers and people who could afford to have a bet.

The way he reported my line about 'living on Sydney
Harbour' irritated me no end. Why? Because all my life I
have been used to nothing flash. All my life I have lived
among salt-of-the-earth people. I have never lived among

multimillionaires, and I never had the desire to. In Sydney, where I have lived for 50 years now, I've lived in Seven Hills, Northmead and Castle Hill. I love those areas and the people who live in them. I worried that this story would give those people the impression that I was yearning for a life with the high-rollers. That was, of course, utter nonsense.

The headline the paper used, too, suggested I had some kind of problem. I wasn't impressed. When I complained to the journo, he said, 'Oh, they changed things after I filed the story. It wasn't my fault.' Bloody wonderful. I was trying to open up and tell what I thought was going to be a nice story for a young pressman, and I got screwed.

For the record, I still have a drink and a bet with my mates – blokes like Dave, Col, Brownie and Sunshine – at the Baulkham Hills Bowling Club. I am in the punters' club, along with them. They're all good blokes, and we all love living in the Hills – as do my mates at the golf club. Some of us could live at Vaucluse but we don't want to!

★

It might sound like a contradiction, given what I have just said, but in the middle and late 1980s, the dark part of my career, my first wife, Monica, thought that perhaps I should do something about my gambling.

'There's a psychiatrist over at North Rocks,' Monica said. 'Why don't you go and see him, and see if he can help you?'

So off I went to see this doctor in North Rocks, and I came away with a strong piece of advice from him: 'Go to the races, but don't drink.'

Right. That Saturday, off I went to Rosehill. I was standing out in an area known as the trainers' bar with my mates, including Phil Gould – that's how far we go back – and his manager, Wayne Beavis. I've met a lot of characters there in the trainers' bar, blokes with nicknames like Louie the Fly and Desperate Dan. Who knows what their real names are! That's racing.

Anyway, we were having our normal Saturday afternoon catch-up. We were telling stories, dirty gags, that sort of thing. But I was following orders and wasn't having a drink. Earlier that morning, I might have spoken to a certain jockey in Melbourne, who had told me about a certain horse that would win in the last. He'd also advised me that the odds on offer would probably blow out, so I shouldn't take the first price available. 'Beautiful,' I'd said. (The bloke tipping the horse will remain nameless, because jockeys aren't supposed to do that, but he's been dead a few years now.)

So, I was standing there at Rosehill, drinking lemon squashes, and in my pocket I had the $200 I was going to put on this horse in the last. Up to this point, it had been the most boring day of my life at the track.

'What's the matter with you?' one of my mates asked.

'Nothing,' I said. 'Just playing it differently.'

As soon as the last race arrived, the first call for the horse I was tipped was 4 to 1. I waited and watched, remembering the old jockey's instructions. Five minutes later, the second call came through: the horse had drifted to 5 to 1 in the ring.

I made my way towards the bookie. There was a crowd to push through and I was nearly to the front, when some big bastard thundered over the top of me. His arm was outstretched, his body odour abounding, and he pushed me to the ground as he claimed the bookie for $2000 to $200 each way.

Needless to say, the bookie hit the knob on his tote board and reeled the horse in from fives to fours. I'd missed the price and I wasn't impressed. Then I looked up from the ground at the bludger who had knocked me over and taken the price.

It was the doctor – the shrink. When I'd seen him earlier that week, I came away thinking he was ordinary. Now I was certain. He had no bedside manner – and no racetrack manners either.

★

Around this time, I'd been calling a lot of provincial racing to make ends meet. On another occasion at the Rosehill trainers' bar, again with Gus and Beavis, I liked a thing called Lee High Lad. I'd seen it win a couple of provincial races and I'd felt that if it came to town, it might just win.

On this day at Rosehill, it was in a weight-for-age race that had only five starters, and there was no hope of it winning this particular race. This event was occupied by millionaires and their horses: the likes of Sir Tristan Antico, Bob Lapointe and the chicken brothers, Jack and Bob Ingham. Lee High Lad was prepared by a hobby trainer, and was rightly rated a 100-to-1 chance.

I never usually played the trifecta, where you pick the first three. But I did this day. I didn't have to outlay a lot of money to cover the various combinations, because there were only five horses.

When they went across the line, Lee High Lad had finished third, and the favourites had finished fourth and fifth. In those days, you had to rely on the on-course announcer to give you the tote prices. 'Here's the interim dividends,' he intoned. 'There's no third dividend. The trifecta's paid $11,240.'

'Shit!' I screamed. '$11,240 bloody dollars!'

There was a kid walking around the bar with a tray. He was dressed in a white shirt and bow tie.

'Hey!' I shouted at him. 'How much are you getting a day to do this?'

'I get $100,' he replied.

'Here's $200,' I told him excitedly. 'Give me the bow tie. You see my circle of friends here? You just look after us.'

The kid couldn't believe it. 'Oh, Jesus, thanks a lot, sir,' he said.

That was when I heard the siren. 'Ladies and gentlemen,' the on-course announcer began. 'There's a protest. Connections of the fifth horse have protested against the third horse, Lee High Lad, for interference between the 300-metre and the 200-metre mark.'

All eyes of our party fell on me, and my head went down like a beaten favourite.

Half an hour later, the dreaded siren wailed again. 'Ladies and gentlemen, the protest has been upheld. The revised placings are: the winner stays in its position, the second horse stays in its position, the fifth horse now becomes the fourth horse, and the fourth horse becomes the third horse.'

In other words, my 100-to-1 shot had been knocked out

by a millionaire – who had already won the fifth-place prize money anyway. Poor old Lee High Lad went back to fifth and I had won nothing.

That was when I started to cry, tears dripping down my cheeks. Gould and Beavis were crying with laughter.

Then the kid came back. 'Can I have my bow tie back?' he asked.

'Sure, and you can keep the $200,' I snorted. My devastation and heartache were written all over my face.

There's a school of thought that racecallers shouldn't gamble on the race they are calling. I've heard it said often, by a lot of other commentators. Personally, I think it's bullshit.

Let's go back to the truly great callers. Bill Collins and Bert Bryant were very big punters, but it didn't affect them as commentators. Bert would say openly during his call, 'I've got my last on this!' And when his horse was beaten, he didn't mind giving them a shellacking. 'It's a fair dinkum pretender!' he'd say. 'Put it on the float and take it home and leave it there.'

Some people reckon they could tell which horse I'd backed in a race. If they did, that's okay with me. All I ever tried to do as a racecaller was paint the picture as accurately and as excitingly as I could. If I was on something, maybe it even added a little bit more excitement. And anyway, when I was punting, I wasn't usually punting big. The other callers might have hundreds on; I might have had a $50 note.

In fact, I reckon there was a distinct advantage of punting and calling, because when I was punting I was doing more research. You've got to watch the videos and study the form. You've got to know that last week a horse carried 59 kilograms, but this week it's only got 55. Last week it drew barrier 13, this week it's got barrier one.

In the moments when you have to ad-lib before the start of a race, it's nice to be able to stand behind the microphone and not have to use notes. Having done all the research for your bets, you can say, 'Well, this should be suited today. It's crying out for the 2400 metres; a fortnight ago it had 59 kilograms, today it's only got 55. It's got a senior jockey . . . '

Of those callers who think it's wrong to bet, there have been several who, because of their lack of knowledge about the gambling side of the industry, fell short of being as good as they could have been, in the eyes of the punters.

Then again, if you're the racecaller and you're in the betting ring when the starters have already jumped, well, that's another problem altogether. That's what happened to me at Gosford one day. I'm pretty sure it's never happened anywhere before or since.

I was the on-course commentator this day, and was in the betting ring talking to the iconic racing journalist Ken Callander; we were working out what we were going to back. I always phoned 'Deafie' – he's deaf in one ear – for tips. Mind you, back then I'd ring anybody. I made more phone calls of a Saturday morning than a telemarketer, I reckon. One time I went to Hong Kong en route to England, and John Jeffs, who had worked at Rosehill and was then the course curator at Sha Tin, organised a lunch for me. I walked into the room and there were half a dozen Hong Kong-based Australian jockeys who all had one thing in common: Rabs ringing them every Saturday morning.

Anyway, that day at Gosford I heard this bloke paging me to go to the broadcasting box. *What do they want?*

I walked over to the bookmaker and had something on this thing called Chippendale, trained by Brian Mayfield-Smith, and owned by Stan and Milly Fox. Ken thought it would win, so I thought it would win, so I backed it.

I strolled up the steps to the broadcasting box. When I get to the top, the chief steward was there. 'Where do you think you've been?' he burst out.

'I've been having a punt,' I replied.

'They've gone halfway!' he bellowed. 'The race is half-over. The people don't know the race is half-over.'

'Oh, shit . . . '

I didn't have time to panic. I turned on the microphone. *'Check, check, one, two. Check, one, two. Ladies and gentlemen, I apologise, we've had a problem with the PA system. They've gone halfway in Race Five, they're at the 800-metre point, and now I'll try and broadcast the race for you. I do apologise, they've gone halfway.'*

Then I realised I didn't know the colours. The only horse I knew was Chippendale, because I'd backed him: he was grey with the purple sleeves and white cap. *'Leaving the 800 metres behind them, Chippendale leads . . .'* And then, looking at the racebook, I called the others, in no particular order.

As they came to the turn, I said to myself, *Jesus, I hope Chippendale stays in front, because I don't know what the others are.* I kept going with my phantom call of everything behind Chippendale. On the turn, the jockey gave it a little bit more rein, and it sprinted three lengths in front. *'Chippendale's extended on the point of the turn and shot three in front,'* I called. *'It's all over, Chippendale will win this, and win in a canter.'*

The whole time I was calling, I had a feeling there was somebody standing behind me. When I got them all across the post, I turned and there was this dear old man who would have been in his 70s. He was retired, and to get a little income he supplied and maintained the PA system at Gosford. It had never broken down in its life, and now he was standing there before me, ashen-faced. His face was the same colour as his hair.

'What's wrong with my PA?' he asked.

'Absolutely nothing, George,' I told him. 'It was either me or the PA to get the blame – I chose the PA.'

'But I'll lose my job!' George said.

'No, you won't,' I told him. 'I'll tell the president what happened and you'll be okay.'

And he was, but the president wasn't impressed with me, let me tell you. For me, the whole episode was a learning curve. You can't ever get complacent. But one of the dark arts of commentating – and I was taught this by Ken Howard – is that when you're calling on the radio, you can get away with some awful lies.

'I'll tell you something, sport,' Ken once said. 'Don't tell the punters what they can't see. If you can't see it, they can't see it. Understand?'

Yes, Ken.

★

The most awful lie I ever told in relation to the evil punt concerned a caravan, a bank manager and the best jockey in the country at the time, 'Miracle' Malcolm Johnston. Any jockey who rode for Tommy Smith was usually considered the best, because he'd be a certainty to win the Sydney jockeys' premiership.

This time I was at Canterbury, and it was a familiar scene: in the car park after the last race, kicking losing betting tickets. That was when I bumped into Malcolm, who had his bag slung over his shoulder and was leaving for the day.

'You look a bit down,' said Miracle, stating the obvious.

'Oh, I've had a prick of a day,' I said.

'We'll get it back tomorrow,' he said. 'I've got five rides at Gosford. They'll all win.'

'Really?' I asked, my eyes lighting up.

Miracle is my mate. He's a real show pony but I love him. I compered his wedding. The next day, I packed up my gear and binoculars and was off to call the races at Gosford, knowing it would be a marvellous, profitable day. I hoped so, at any rate, since I'd dropped a fair sum at Canterbury.

I saw Miracle before the first. The horse he was riding was at 9 to 4. 'We'll win easily,' he told me. I had a really good bet on it, then climbed the steps to the broadcast box, feeling confident about the result.

It was a mile race, but at the first turn the bit pulled through the mouth of Malcolm's horse. He had no control and was headed for the outside rail. After trying desperately to ensure that his mount didn't go through the rail and towards a nearby bowling green, which was occupied by a hundred or so bowlers, Miracle pulled the horse up.

I'd done more money, and my debt from the last two days was reaching horrific proportions. I was betting with the same bookmaker – Jeff Pendlebury – and every time I backed a loser he looked at me as if to say, 'Do you know what you're doing?'

Before the next race I went down to the mounting yard to see Miracle. 'Sorry about that,' he said.

'Yeah, so am I.'

'This horse is 6 to 4 – it can't get beaten.'

'Fair enough.'

I walked back to Pendlebury in the betting ring again and had twice as much on Miracle's mount. It ran third. Now my account had gone up even higher. Again I confronted Malcolm.

'I'm almost too frightened to say this,' said the little bloke. 'This one really *can't* get beat.'

Back I went to Pendlebury's stand, and I doubled again. I was working on the theory that if I kept doubling, I'd have to back a winner sooner or later. This time, Pendlebury asked the question outright: 'Mate, do you know what you're doing?'

Calling these races was becoming increasingly stressful. I was trying to remember the colours, but at the same time I was watching every move Miracle made, my debits increasing . . .

Can't get beat? It ran fourth. The next horse was no good either.

Finally we came to the last race. 'I'm having an awful day,' Miracle told me.

'So am I,' I said. 'Penniless, broke and hurting.'

'Well, this last one will win,' he said.

'Mate, you've been saying that all day.'

'Yeah, but, mate, they *can't* beat this one.'

The last event on the card at Gosford this day was a 1000-metre sprint, with a big, precocious-looking thing called

Sobers. It was big and black, trained by Paul Sutherland and owned by John Austin. I can still see its colours: pale blue with white braces.

'What price?' Miracle asked me.

'It's 5 to 2,' I told him.

'It should be odds-on.'

I rushed back to Pendlebury on the nod and doubled again. This time I put on enough to clear my entire debt. If the horse won, I'd be square. If Sobers got beaten, I'd owe him no less than $8000. Shit!

Up I went to the broadcast box. *'Racing! Sobers began like a bullet from the outside, and Johnston immediately brings it over to the rails. Lovely piece of horsemanship . . . They come to the turn, and Johnston has got this horse Sobers absolutely bolting. He's about to ask it to go now . . . And Sobers. . . well, there's nothing there! It's gone! Sobers is gone! It's gone from cantering to stone motherless last in the twinkling of an eye . . . Last home is Sobers.'*

I didn't see Miracle after the race. As I drove home, all I could think was: *How am I going to pay for this?* A crazy idea came into my mind: I'll go visit my mate 'Tails' at the bank. The next day, off I went, and I asked Tails if I could have a word in his office.

'I need $8000, mate,' I explained. 'I've got an opportunity

to buy a caravan right on the water at Umina at Ocean Beach. I need a personal loan.'

'Sweet,' said Tails, leaning over to write out a cheque. 'Your credit is good. Where did you say it is? Umina?'

'Easts Caravan Park,' I replied. 'Ocean Beach.'

'That's incredible!' said Tails. 'The mother-in-law's got a caravan there too. We're going up there in three or four weeks' time. I'll come around and have a beer!'

'Yeah, that's good,' I said. 'I'll throw a bit of steak and some sausages on the barbie.' It was a blatant lie: there was no caravan. I walked out of the bank and straight into the post office next door, where I sent the cheque to Pendlebury. So I'd paid the debt back to my bookie, but now I had to pay back the bank.

I know! I thought, and I walked around the corner to the National Australia Bank, which had a sign up in the window: 'Personal loans 8% p/a.' I walked in and enquired about another loan. The bank manager asked what I did for work.

'I'm a sports broadcaster,' I told him. 'I'm an understudy racecaller at 2GB.'

'You'd know Johnny Tapp then?' he said.

'Yeah, I work with him.'

'Ken Howard?'

'Yeah, I know Ken Howard.'

'What can I do for you?'

'I want to buy a caravan at Umina,' I said. 'It's a nice caravan on the water. I need $8000.'

'Good as gold. What's your full name and address?' After getting all my details, he wrote me a cheque for $8000.

Instead of walking back around the corner to the Commonwealth Bank, I decided to let things sit for a couple of days. After a week I went back to the Commonwealth Bank. By then I'd banked NAB's cheque and written out my own. I went back to see Tails.

'You know that caravan at Umina?' I told him. 'You won't believe it. I worked on it last weekend. I got the scrubbing brush out and gave it a schmick-up, put a sign in the office window with my phone number and in 24 hours I had an offer I couldn't refuse. I got $10,000 for it. A profit of $2000!'

'You're a genius!' he declared. 'So we won't be having that beer?'

'Well, no, I haven't got a caravan. I've sold the barbie as well.'

'Oh, well, that's bad luck. Why don't you come up to Mum's caravan anyway and have a barbie there?'

'Lovely idea, Tails,' I said. 'I'll see you then.'

'Miracle' Malcolm Johnston is the worst tipster I've met.

The only winner he ever tipped me was the Tommy Smith champion Kingston Town, when it was 40 to 1 on. After what I'd lost on Mal's tips at Gosford that day, I'd have to have bet some $320,000 on the King to win back my $8000!

★

My gambling may have been out of control for a brief period. I was so hurt by what happened at Ten that I just went off the rails for a while. It happens!

There was a time when people thought I owned the Northmead TAB, I was there so often. It was the meeting place for all my mates. The boys just loved it. We'd get a couple of slabs of beer from Chris and Grace Sampson in the bottle shop – lovely people – and spend the entire day at the TAB. Once, when I lost my kelpie, I went up to the TAB and there she was. She knew where I'd be. She'd had to cross two main roads to get there.

I become irate with politicians who insist the amount of money a person puts through a poker machine should be capped. What they don't understand is that the gambler they're trying to help – the problem gambler – will just turn to something else if he's still got money in his pocket. He'll turn to Keno, or he'll turn to the TAB, or he'll find a game of cards. He will get rid of his money one way or another, because that's his problem – he can't help himself. He's a problem gambler.

I will tell anybody who wants to listen that I've punted for seven decades and I know you can't win. I don't know anybody who wins. Bookmakers drive Mercedes-Benzes, and those who own the corporate agencies are all filthy rich. I've had this conversation with lots of young blokes who I knew had gambling problems.

You can tell them how they can't win but they don't listen. While they have money in their pockets they will get rid of it. Capping the pokies is only a brief bandaid solution; there are many other ways they can lose their dough.

There's no way you're going to get rid of gambling across the board. If you try, it will go back underground – and you know what that means.

Simply, problem gamblers, like those addicted to drugs and alcohol, need help. They are suffering from an illness. They need medical assistance, counselling, all of that – not just capping a bloody poker machine.

12

A TOE IN THE WATER

At football clubs, when one door closes another one opens. Players come and go, and opportunities for new players depend on whether there's a space available. Spots in the commentary box are much the same. When Ian Maurice – or 'the Bear', as he is affectionately known – left Channel Nine in 1989 to join Ten, he was replacing Rex Mossop, who had replaced me at Ten four years earlier. Ian's move opened the door for me to call State of Origin football for the first time in my career.

I'd never called Origin, the interstate series between New South Wales and Queensland that had first sparked in 1980, and which has gone on to become the jewel in rugby league's crown. But I had watched it, of course. I'd sat back and watched and listened and thought, *How good is this?*

That was probably because of the bloke who was calling it. He was the Nine institution with the booming voice that made mine seem like a choirboy's. Legend has it that the director of sport during the 1980s, David Hill, would stand behind this commentator with a rolled-up newspaper and whack him continuously to make sure his excitement levels remained high for the entire broadcast.

His name was Darrell Eastlake, almost everything that happened was HUGE! For many years he was as Origin as Lang Park, Wally Lewis, Steve Mortimer and a fight in the first five minutes.

Alongside Darrell and the legendary coach Jack Gibson, I called Origins and some Test matches in New Zealand. I was like a kid in a candy shop, because I was back, even though it was in a casual capacity. I went to some football matches and called some games to myself in preparation. I felt the skills returning; it was like riding a bike.

It wasn't rugby league that opened the door for my possible return to commentary on a full-time basis, but another sport, and alongside another legendary caller. That sport was swimming, and the caller was Norman May – or 'Nugget', as everyone knew him.

By the late 1980s Nugget was an Australian radio and television sports broadcasting icon. He was best known for his call of the men's 4 x 100-metre medley final at the 1980 Olympic Games in Moscow: *'Gold! Gold for Australia! Gold!'* Having started at the ABC in 1954, he had retired from full-time work in 1984 – meaning he'd spent 30 years behind the microphone – but he wasn't ready to quit altogether.

So, after Nine bought the broadcast rights to the 1990 Commonwealth Games in Auckland, New Zealand, they paired us up. Nugget had a glass eye, courtesy of a bow-and-arrow game gone wrong when he was a kid of six, growing up in Sydney's eastern suburbs. Now his good eye was fading. Nine needed someone to call the races, with Nugget doing the expert analysis.

We called two national championships, in Perth in 1989 and then in Adelaide in 1990, which doubled as selection trials for Auckland. The likes of Lisa Curry-Kenny, Andrew Baildon and Karen van Wirdum were the headline acts of the pool around this time, along with an unassuming long-distance swimmer from Queensland called Glen Housman. I nicknamed him the 'Paperboy', because that's what he looked like. He broke 15 minutes at the selection trials, obliterating the world record, but the record was disallowed because the electronic timing equipment failed as he touched the finishing wall. It was a travesty: he was clearly ahead of the world record as he touched.

Some people say I call swimming like it's football. In reality, it's nothing to do with football – it's a throwback to my racing days. I'd rolled the marbles as a kid, I'd called three Melbourne Cups, and this was a return to both of those things.

For me, swimmers were like horses: they were either a body-length away from one another, or a half-metre in front and so on. They didn't have colours but they raced in lanes, which made it even easier. I can't ever remember a swimmer starting in lane two and finishing in lane three!

I'd never called swimming before in my life, but in calling the nationals I must have made some sort of impression. I was on the plane to Auckland.

I sat alongside Nugget on the flight over, and the trip set the tone for what lay ahead. He'd done some sort of contra deal with Bollinger, and the expensive champagne was flowing freely. Qantas is a lovely airline, but it was never this generous. We imbibed – a lot. As I would discover, anyone who came onto the Nine set throughout those games would leave with a bottle of Bollinger.

It was intimidating working with a legend. I had three research books – each one an inch thick – that I'd prepared, but Norman carried not one page. It was all in his head. He knew splits, he knew world records, he knew what time was required by any given swimmer to qualify for a semi-final or a final or to win. He knew everything. How? I don't know.

When we arrived, we checked into the Travelodge down on the harbour, and it turned out the pair of us had an interconnecting room. That was great because I could call out and ask him a question at any given time when I was doing my research for the upcoming day of swimming.

Shortly after we arrived, I went into his room and saw his suitcase open on his bed. It was impeccably packed. I noticed there were 14 handkerchiefs, 14 pairs of socks, 14 well-pressed shirts and ties, and so on. They were all neatly compartmentalised.

'What's with all the clothes?' I asked him.

'Mate, we haven't got any time for washing and ironing,' he said. 'We're going to be very busy.'

'The swimming can't be that busy, surely?'

'No, no, no. Mate, we've got a lot of booze to drink.'

Norman, as you can probably tell, didn't mind a drink. After night one of the action, we assembled back at the hotel bar with the crew and had about four schooners. The two of us then went to dinner in the adjoining restaurant.

'Two bottles of your best red,' he said to the waiter.

'I don't drink red,' I said.

'I haven't ordered for you,' he fired back.

Australia completely dominated the swimming program in Auckland. The games saw the emergence of Hayley Lewis, who won five gold medals. Nicole Stevenson established herself as the backstroke queen. Susie O'Neill was just coming on.

Housman duly won the 1500 metres, which helped to ease the disappointment of the national titles when he was denied his world record. At around the 800-metre mark of the final, though, Norman gave another young Australian a significant endorsement. He said that 'this kid' Kieren Perkins was someone to watch.

In the end, the Australian swim team smashed it at those Commonwealth Games. They won 21 gold medals, and on every occasion Norman stood and sang the national anthem, waving the Australian and boxing kangaroo flags at the same time.

★

For me, though, despite the Australian swimmers' success, the most memorable call from those games related to a Zambian.

One morning, Norman and I were sitting back and watching the heats of the men's 200-metre breaststroke. We only had to call the prominent Australians when they appeared. We had our feet on the desk. I was smoking in those days, so I was puffing away. It was all very boring. Then we came to heat 33.

There were four entrants on the sheet: one from the Isle of Wight, another from Guernsey, another from Jersey and the last one from Zambia. Only one swimmer walked out onto the pool deck: the kid from Zambia. His name was Richard Shombay. You could not find a slower event than the 200-metre breaststroke.

Suddenly, the phone at our desk rang. It was the producer. 'Put your headphones on!' he said. 'Quickly! They want you to call this bloke.'

This has to be a gee-up, I thought. But it wasn't.

So I sparked into action. '*Here's Richard Shombay, about to go through the hundred metres . . .*' I'd never before called a one-man swimming event. I'd never called a one-man anything! I was struggling for words. *'He's coming up to the 100-metre mark, he's halfway, and looking at that split time he's about 15 seconds outside the world record . . .'*

Norman couldn't help himself. *'Yeah, but he might have a big back half, Ray.'*

Thanks for that, Nugget.

'Well, Shombay, he might be outside world record time, but this must still be quite a thrill for the young man, even though he's alone there in the pool . . .' It was a classic case of patter, ad-lib, bullshit and gibber. I got Shombay over the line, and then it was down to the pool deck to Anne-Maree Sparkman for the post-race interview.

This was where things got tricky. At our very first production meeting, all the on-air talent was told that if we asked an athlete one particular question during an interview – 'How do you feel?' – we would be on the first flight back to Sydney.

'Is this your first international success?' Anne-Maree asked.

'Yes,' was the detailed reply from Richard, who was breathing heavily after the heat he had so convincingly won.

'You must be the hero of the Zambian team right now?'

'There's only me in it.'

Anne-Maree kept trying. 'When did you realise you had the race won?'

'When nobody else showed up.'

As an interview, that was GOLD, GOLD, GOLD!

I was away for Australia Day during those Commonwealth Games. I missed Cher and her family becoming Australian citizens that day, too. But I developed a passion for swimming in Auckland, and it opened the door for me to call much more of it later in my career.

It also opened the door for something more critical than that. Jim Fitzpatrick was the head of sport at Nine at the time. At the Nine cast and crew party after the closing ceremony, he pulled me aside. 'We'll have to do something with you,' he said.

In other words: *We'll keep you in mind for the future.*

I know that certain people on that trip were urging Nine management to find a gig for me. I wasn't holding my breath, but it was good to feel wanted again.

When I got back to Sydney, it took me several weeks to recover. Believe it or not, I've managed to dodge Nugget ever since – but not because I dislike him. To the contrary, I love him, but he's too bloody dangerous! God, he liked a drink. I should point out that it never affected his performance, and he never drank on the job.

In the 2011 book *Back to the Studio*, written by Peter Meares, Nugget said this of me:

> His sense of theatre, combined with a great voice, enable him to capture the most exciting moments brilliantly. He's a great commercial caller. Just as he lifts his excitement level for the last 25 metres of an Ian Thorpe swim, so the newsroom can replay the best 'grab' for their bulletin, he does the same in football when a try is on. No matter what you're doing, you've just got to watch – and that's great broadcasting.

That really was an amazing compliment, from an amazing commentator. In fact, in my view, Norman May was simply the best, but I thank you, Nugget.

13

BIG DAZ AND BIG JACK

Darrell Eastlake is one of those characters who will always stand out in the crowd, not only because of his size but also because of that big raucous nature of his. Working with him was fun but also scary. He had a persona that always seemed to attract the lunatics.

The representative games were pretty much the only footy that Big D did. A walk around Lang Park with Darrell on Origin night was a nightmare. What the fans called him wasn't very funny, and nor was what they threw at him, so after a couple of occasions I chose to walk the other way. It was safer.

Eastlake, like all of us in this business, copped his share of baggers, but I can assure you he turned some of the most boring sports into frenzied excitement. I still don't know what he said some of the time, but I do know this: I never watched weightlifting until Darrell started commentating on it. He attracted many people – not to the sport, but to listen to him absolutely losing it.

As I put this book together, Darrell is not in the best of health. I pray for him, and I remember very fondly all the fun we had together.

We were in New Zealand when he introduced me to the viewers of *Wide World of Sports* in the late 1980s. We were in Auckland for a Test match, and it was my first appearance on Nine. He thought it would be nice to introduce me to the viewers on the Saturday-afternoon flagship, which was hosted by Ian Chappell and Ken Sutcliffe back in Australia.

Sure enough, I got introduced to the all-important Saturday program precisely as the skies opened. We were standing in the middle of Eden Park. When Eastlake set the scene and turned to me, he looked like the Loch Ness Monster. You should have seen him: hair washing down his face, make-up cascading down the furrows of his brow, his big mouth spitting out copious amounts of words and water.

Anyone within two metres was getting a double spray, but then, as I looked down at the monitor, I realised that yours truly looked like his twin brother. It was ugly. I thought

Eastlake looked hideous, but compared to me he looked like Cary Grant. I've no doubt this is the precise moment when Nine started to make preparations to have me on camera as infrequently as possible.

In many ways, I'm sure this has actually prolonged my television career. Strange, isn't it? When I'm asked how I have lasted so long on TV, the answer has to be: 'By not being seen.'

Needless to say, our clothes were soon drenched. If Eastlake told me once, he told me four times that his jacket was from New York and was the best thing he'd ever bought – a combination of mohair and something else, I seem to recall him saying. He loved it like his Harley-Davidson. I didn't really care about mine – it was one that Channel Ten had supplied me and that I didn't particularly like anyway.

Eastlake took both our jackets to the dry-cleaners. When they came back, you should have seen his face. His jacket now looked like it was meant for one of the seven dwarfs. It had shrunk to half its original size, but he still tried to make it fit him. The sleeves came up to his elbows, and the lapels had curled up like cabbage leaves. It was stuffed.

He was devastated, and he screamed and ranted and threatened. It was like the end of his world had arrived. The last thing I knew, he was heading off with both his and my jacket in the direction of some insurance company, in search of retribution.

That was the first of two jackets he lost on that trip. On another day he was recording the opener for a Test match in Rotorua. Naturally, he wanted to do it standing in front of the hot springs and geysers. They're stinking bloody things, reeking of sulphur, and he'd been warned to stay out of their way when a siren sounded – it meant they were about to blow.

So there he was, his make-up done, dressed like Versace, and then they counted him in: 'Five, four, three, two, one . . . Cue!'

Big Darrell was killing them, setting the scene for the Test match, when suddenly the geyser went off. It blew like a surfacing whale, spewing mud and slush and water hundreds of feet into the air. Naturally, what goes up must come down, and guess where it landed? Right on Darrell's sizeable head and jacket.

This time, there was no visit to the cleaners. This jacket had been invaded by the smell of sulphur, and that's something you just can't get rid of. Poor bloody Eastlake. He only took two jackets on the trip and both finished up in the garbage. They say there's a Kiwi dwarf still wearing the mohair one from New York.

★

At that Test match in Rotorua, Darrell did the on-camera introductions from the dressing-rooms. Some big Maori blokes on the hill had been giving it to him all day long. From the time he walked into the ground and found the broadcast box, they were at him: 'Go home, you big mug! What would you know about anything, you git?' At one stage Daz stood up to comb his hair before going on camera and they had a one-liner ready to go: 'Why don't you take it off and comb it, you mug?'

When the game came to an end, Jack Gibson and I went onto the landing outside the commentary box to do the closing piece after Darrell had interviewed the man of the match. The floor manager started putting our earpieces in place. The microphones had been left on the floor of the landing as we got ready to do the cross.

Unbeknown to me, the Maoris had got under the landing, grabbed the mic leads and tied them to the scaffolding that was holding the whole structure up. The floor manager sang out, 'Thirty seconds, Rabs, and they want no more than two minutes' wrap.'

I leant down to pick up the mic and bring it to my mouth, but it wouldn't budge off the floor. I could hear the director,

Geoff Morris, screaming out, 'Where's Rabs? Ten seconds! Where is the bloody clown?'

The floor manager was trying to tell him what had happened. In the meantime, I heard 'Cue Rabs!' So I dropped down onto the floor and started talking into the mic. Big Jack was okay, because his mic hadn't been tied up. The director just took some wide shots of the fans making their way home, while I was on the floor rambling on about the game until someone managed to untie the bloody cord.

In hindsight, it was pretty funny. The Maoris thought they'd set up Big D, but in reality they had snared me in their trap.

Gibbo loved it. 'You seem to work better when you're on your hands and knees, Rabs,' he said, ever so dryly.

'Yes, Jack,' I smirked. 'Very funny.'

Jack Gibson was the supercoach, a man who changed the game. He won back-to-back premierships with Eastern Suburbs in 1974 and 1975, and then three with the Eels from 1981 to 1983. His commentary with Nine opened him up to a whole new – and younger – audience.

But his coaching ability was only part of the story. He was just so interesting. His manner, his sense of humour and his passion for the game made him almost irresistible as a person.

Jack didn't do anything extraordinary, mainly because, as he would tell you, rugby league is not an extraordinary game. Rather, he would say, it is a simple game made difficult by those who try to over-teach it. One of his lines was to do the simple things well, and the rest will look after itself.

Fans of the game know him for his one-liners, mainly during Origin games alongside Big Darrell. 'They'd boo Santa Claus, this mob,' he once said of the Queensland crowd. Or this, of NSW winger Andrew Ettingshausen: 'ET is so quick he can turn the light out and be in bed before the light goes out.'

On our trips to and from New Zealand, I'd sit next to him on the flight. He'd pull out his clipboard and start making notes in his beautiful, sloping longhand. I was trying to look but not be noticed. He was writing down his one-liners, ready to be brought out at any stage of a match broadcast.

His offsider, Ron Massey, also was a man full of impact. I don't know how much Gibson relied on Massey, or if it was the other way around, but as two people working together they had amazing chemistry. Big Jack passed away in the hour before the Centenary Test at the SCG in 2008, after a long battle with dementia. That was a tough night for me and Peter Sterling, who was in the box next to me. Sterlo had been shaped by the supercoach during their premiership years together at Parramatta.

Ron remains a wonderful friend. I will never forget standing at the pulpit to deliver Dad's eulogy in 1996. I looked out over the congregation, and there was Ron and his wife, sitting at the back of the church. They'd driven 300 miles to Junee, just to represent the league at Dad's farewell. Even now, every time I'm about to call a big match, 'Mass' will phone me to wish me luck.

That said, when I had to interview Massey and Jack together, I turned to jelly. Throw in Jimmy Connors and John McEnroe, and you've got my four most terrifying interviewees of all time.

I've met some great people through rugby league – some giants of the game. In fact, if it wasn't for those people, the game couldn't possibly have survived as it has.

I've never known any sport to have the troubles of this game and survive. One of league's major problems stems from the clubs. They vote or push for whatever is best for them. They don't seem to think of the game first. It's always them first, and the others and the game can fend for themselves.

When the Super League idea came along in the mid-1990s, it only got off the ground because some clubs saw it as a better avenue for them. Not a better avenue for the game generally, but a better way for them.

The formation of the independent Australian Rugby League Commission in 2012 was an important step for the game that is allowing it to move away from this self-interest. But I do know one thing: when people start putting the game first, that's when it will make its giant leap forward.

Apart from clubs, there have also been individuals who seem to think they are bigger than the game. Their egos prevent them from putting anything else in front of their own ambition.

There have been some significant people of influence, too. Peter 'Bullfrog' Moore's involvement with Super League may have tarnished his reputation with those from the Australian Rugby League, but no one could deny that he had huge power. At the end of his tenure with the Bulldogs, he is reported to have said, in answer to the News Limited offer, 'It's too good to turn our backs on but I will leave it with you people to work through.'

Kevin Humphreys – who was chairman of the NSWRL during the 1970s and early 1980s – ruled the game with an iron fist. He had an almost dictatorial presence. I'm still not sure that wasn't the best way for him to go. He didn't need cumbersome committees bulging at the seams. John Quayle – who ran the game from the mid-1980s to the 1990s – is someone for whom I have an enormous amount of time. I wish he was still involved in a larger capacity.

Quayle became general manager alongside chairman Ken 'Arko' Arthurson, who in many ways was quite like Kevin. He was one of the Humphreys men, and, after leading Manly to much success, eventually took over the league. Ken's manner was a bit different, though. He was always the strategic diplomat. The ultimate manipulator. On one occasion, those skills saved my life.

During the 1970s, I led a couple of footy tours to England and France, and one of my offsiders on one of these excursions was Arko. He was great company. On one trip, we had a stopover in the Mexican town of Taxco on our way from Mexico City to Acapulco. After a couple of tequilas at the hotel, Arko and I headed off to explore the nightlife.

We finished up at someone's party. We were quite uninvited but no one seemed to object to us being there. Well, not until I started leering at some Mexican beauty on the other side of the dance floor. Perving, you might say. I turned away and resumed talking to Arko, when suddenly an anxious look came across the Manly supremo's face. He was looking straight past me.

'Rabs, don't turn around,' he advised. 'Just start walking to the exit. I think we're in a bit of trouble.'

There must have been seven of them, and nearly all were armed with something, including broken bottles. This girl's partner and his mates weren't happy chappies. Once we reached the door, Arko and I bolted. He could really run, but the gap between the gang and me was narrowing.

That's when I learnt that Arko was solid. Even though he was a mile in front of me, he stopped and came back. 'You keep going,' he said. 'I'll try to reason with them.'

'Kenny! You're mad!'

But I'd forgotten one thing: he was always a top negotiator. There was never a player he wanted whom he didn't get. Now he was negotiating for my freedom and good health.

I don't know what he said; all I know is that the lynch mob was no longer chasing us. Somehow, Arko had pacified them. I'm surprised none of them ended up playing for Manly.

14

THE COMEBACK

During my years in exile, I made a deal with myself: if I ever came back, I wasn't going to go out of my way to be Mr Nice Guy any longer. I'd been replaced at Ten by Rex Mossop because his way of giving his opinion bordered on arrogance. In commercial television, that was a major plus, and the time I spent on the outside looking in allowed me to realise as much.

In fact, Jack Gibson also brought this issue to my attention. 'You know, Ray,' he told me in his trademark drawl, 'your biggest problem is that you try to be friends with everyone. And you can't.'

That was during the darkest period in my life, in the year or so after the 1986 Grand Final. Jack was saying that my fence-sitting came over in my commentary: that it was too sanitised. In other words, I didn't bag anybody because I didn't want any rough water.

That was the Ken Howard way, and it was how Johnny Tapp and I had been trained to call: *If you can't say something nice, don't say anything at all.* But calling football is different to calling a race. You have to be robust. So I made a promise to myself that if I ever earned the chance to call football full-time again, I would have an opinion, although I'd always keep it respectful.

Although by the turn of the decade I was working for Nine on a casual basis, I remained pessimistic that I'd ever earn another shot as a permanent commentator. My sons, Mark and Chris, had kept reassuring me I would. 'Don't worry,' they'd say. 'It will come back to you. You'll get back.'

'Maybe,' I'd reply. 'Perhaps.'

In November 1991 they were proven right. The phone buzzed, and on the other end was Ian Frykberg, Channel Nine's larger-than-life head of sport and current affairs and one of Kerry Packer's most trusted lieutenants. 'How would you like to call football again?' he asked. 'Full-time.'

'I'd love to,' I said.

'How long do you need to think about it?'

'Five seconds.'

You could put it down to serendipity. Channel Ten, along with Seven, had been placed into receivership in 1990. Ten was shedding programs, with the exception of *Neighbours*, and the rugby league coverage from which I had been punted was back on the market. Realising the advertising dollars on offer, especially with the advent of Friday-night football, Channel Nine snapped up the rights.

The irony was that for the whole time I worked at Ten, I really wanted to be at Nine. Why? Because they were the best. Ken Howard had worked there. John Tapp worked there. This was the station that had created the careers of Graeme Kennedy and Bert Newton. In Sydney, Brian Henderson read the 6 pm nightly news. 'Brian told me' was the catchcry. People still know what that means, and that's because he was on Channel Nine. They were the best.

To understand how much I wanted to work at Nine, you only need to go into my wardrobe at home. That's where you will find a jumper that explains it all.

When I worked casually for Nine in 1989, calling Origin with Darrell Eastlake, everyone on the outside broadcast crew had a Channel Nine jumper, with the iconic logo featuring the nine dots. I didn't have one, though, because I was a casual employee. So I went into a store one day, bought a similar jumper, then went to Nine's wardrobe department. 'Is there any way you can get me one of those Channel Nine logos, like a patch?' I asked.

'Oh, yeah,' they said. 'Not a problem.'

I went home and sewed it on myself, and from then on I wouldn't go to work without it, even in the middle of summer. To this day, I can't throw it out. That's what Channel Nine meant to me then, and still does.

Ian Frykberg's call came with a rider. 'I'm leaving,' he said. 'I'm going to work for Murdoch.' As in Rupert Murdoch, whose News Limited ran Sydney's *Daily Telegraph* and was now about to venture into the electronic media. Pay television hadn't yet arrived in Australia, but it was firmly on News's horizon.

Frykers was a massive man with a massive heart, and he turned out to be a great mentor and a great mate early on in my time at Nine, but his replacement turned out to be just as 'user-friendly', as he said. Gary Burns became an equally important ally for me as Frykers.

Assembling the commentary team to be built around

me was the first task. Darrell Eastlake was to be a part of it, naturally, but we also needed expert callers and sideline eyes. Frykers asked me what I thought of Peter Sterling, the premiership-winning Parramatta playmaker who had recently retired and who had done some sideline work for Ten before it went bust.

I had known Sterlo for years but we weren't close. To say we were great mates then would be wrong, but in time we became just that. He had lived around the corner from me at Northmead in the Hills district of north-west Sydney when he was a 17-year-old playing first grade for Parramatta.

I certainly knew how good he had been as a player. At one stage I considered him the best player I had seen; that was a mantle that changed hands throughout my years as a caller.

When I first arrived in Sydney, the first player I saw was Manly's Bob Fulton. I didn't see John Raper or Reg Gasnier, the St George greats, so when I came through Fulton was my idol. Suddenly, I was wondering how Fulton lined up against Graeme Langlands, the great Dragons fullback. Then Graham Eadie came through. Then I saw Sterling, the greatest thing since sliced bread. Then Allan Langer, the Broncos halfback, superseded him. Then there was Wally Lewis, the Queensland legend, and then there was Andrew

Johns, possibly the greatest ever. Over a long period of time, there have been plenty of blokes on my throne. Sterlo was one of them.

'He'd be great,' I told Frykberg. 'Sign him up.'

One of the first things Burns did after he replaced Frykberg was appoint Paul Vautin to the commentary team. 'Fatty' was already well known on television: not so much for his deeds on the field for Manly, Queensland or Australia, or for his red hair, but rather for his work on *The Midday Show with Ray Martin*. He had goofed around on-air for a few years with cricketer Simon O'Donnell. Burnsy was the executive producer of *Midday*, and could see then the value in having someone with a humorous side on Nine's football coverage.

An instant chemistry formed between Sterlo and Fatty, and the 1992 Tooheys Challenge – the preseason competition for the Winfield Cup – gave us the perfect opportunity to get to know each other better. It also gave me a chance to travel with the pair of them in a car, from country town to country town around New South Wales, with our golf clubs in the back.

That was a buzz – really good fun. We'd do Albury on a Saturday, then they'd go off to the airport. I'd drive over to Junee, see Mum and Dad, and then drive on to Bega. I had no idea which motel we'd be staying in, but I knew I'd find Sterling and Vautin at the local TAB. I'd go there and, lo and behold, there they'd be.

The match would be played in daylight-savings time, and half an hour after full-time we'd be on the golf course. In those days, neither of them could play. They were just learning the game. They were playing off handicaps of about 24, while I was off 13. The country courses we played on were quite tight, so I won a bit of money off them in those days.

I'd leave my driver in my bag and just use a five-iron, while these two blokes, with their expensive new sticks, would be plonking wayward drives straight into the creeks and bushes where the brown and red-bellied black snakes were. I just kept putting more and more money into my pocket.

The worm has now turned: these days Fatty plays off four, Sterling's off nine and I've drifted to 14.

We had some great times, and in a short space of time became great mates. They also steered me into plenty of trouble. One of the matches of that preseason was in Armidale, in the northern tablelands of New South Wales. The day before the game Gary Burns called a production meeting. 'Your punctuality is abhorrent,' he told the three of us. 'As of today, if you can't get there on time, don't bother coming.'

The next day, however, the Lee Freedman-trained champion horse Super Impose was racing, chasing some sort of equine record. Naturally, Vautin and Sterling were punting on the whole race meeting. Fatty was walking around the hotel we were staying at with TAB tickets an inch thick in his top pocket.

It was time for us to go – but Super Impose hadn't raced.

'Fellas,' I cautioned. 'We're on a warning. Can we go?'

'They're just reshoeing a thing at the barrier,' they chirped back.

'Okay, don't listen to me,' I said. 'Don't tell me I didn't warn you.'

I was in the car as they watched the race. I was a nervous wreck because I wanted to get to the ground. I was always the driver – not that they ever thanked me.

When we finally got on the road we were running a bit late. We approached the ground, and we could see the scaffolding on which the local ground management had erected a temporary commentary box. That was where we'd be calling the game.

I let Fatty and Sterlo out in advance, while I parked the car miles away in an adjacent paddock. The pair of them were two minutes late, but I came in a distant third, about ten minutes after them. When I climbed into the box, Burns gave me the best spray of all time.

'You've been watching the races, haven't you?' he bellowed. 'Super Impose?'

Vautin and Sterling had 'forgotten' to tell Gary that I was parking the car. In fact, as I learnt soon enough, they had even told him that they'd made their own way to the ground. Bastards!

That's how it was for a lot of years. Sterlo and Fatty and plenty of jokes at my expense. I was subjected to wrong teams, wrong changes to the line-ups, wrong referees' names, sandwiches stuffed in my headphones and many other pranks. Strangely, though, I think they still like me.

When I think about it, they actually did me a favour. They loosened me up. Before working with them at Nine, I worried about calling players incorrectly – I'd bash myself up for a week. Sterling and Vautin would take the mickey out of me before the match had even finished, so the press couldn't get at me. They didn't hesitate to highlight any mistakes. The first thing Fatty would say was 'Give yourself an uppercut!' or 'Turn it up!' We called the football with self-deprecating humour.

Working this way was like nothing I had ever done before. It made me feel like one of the boys. It made me feel younger. And it made me realise that calling games of rugby league should be fun. Anybody can make a mistake. As long as you haven't got the winger who just scored the try wrong, or the score, it's not the end of the world.

For the Sunday match, Nine tried to edit the match back to an hour of TV time, which equates to about 42 minutes of football. I was amazed at the job the editor, Peter Geon, did. He was called 'Lucky', and he had to be. He had some impossible missions to edit a match down and get it to air at 6.30 pm. That broadcast copped a lambasting from the media at the time, who said what a joke it was.

Darrell pulled the pin fairly early on. Weekly football was different to Origin, and his booming style was better suited to that: big and raucous. When you heard Darrell call 'HUGE!' in a match between Wests and Illawarra in Wollongong, it wasn't quite the same as New South Wales and Queensland at Lang Park! Sunday football also stopped him from doing his surfing, and it meant him giving up calling the Formula One, so he quit.

Steve Roach, the big Balmain prop, joined us as a sideline eye, and the little North Sydney hooker Tony Rae also did some work for us. His nickname was 'Clouds'. Why? One day he was doing a live cross, and he said: 'Yes, beautiful day here. Gorgeous day, not a cloud in the sky.' At that very moment, a dirty great cloud was floating across the sky behind him.

I'd love to take everyone inside the commentary box. Sterling has always delighted in the gee-up. One of his favourites is to confuse me about pronunciations. Is it Dean Tree-ster or Try-ster? Is it Steve Ren-oof or Ren-off? Bar-tolo or Bartol-o?

One weekend, we were covering the World Sevens tournament. Someone had come up with the idea of inviting teams from Russia, America, Japan and even Morocco to compete against our own sides, plus teams from Tonga, Fiji, Papua New Guinea and New Zealand. The concept looked good on paper but died a natural death.

Anyway, on this occasion I was commentating a game between a Sydney side and Russia. The visitors had names like Volkov, Raminov, Piskov and, believe it or not, Pharkov. It had to be a gee-up – but it wasn't. So I treated the Russians just as I had the lads from Port Moresby at Lang Park many years before. I called this game seven minutes each way and not once did I dare call Pharkov's name. I simply dismissed him from the commentary.

The scoreline was embarrassing: the Sydney side led by 50 or more, and the crowd was begging for a Russian try. Suddenly, they made a break.

'*Volkov to Raminov, inside to Skirskov, now it's with Ustinov . . .*'

Next the ball went out to Pharkov, who ran through and scored the Russians' first try. Out of good taste, though, I called him Krushev instead. I mean, the match wasn't going live to Moscow. I doubted that the people of Russia even knew they were represented, and their chances of seeing a replay was about 2 million to 1. No one knew, no one cared – except for Perfect Peter.

So Sterlo piped up, having said nothing all game. Perhaps he didn't even realise I was doing a phantom call. 'Ray, I hate to correct you,' he said. 'But number four was Pharkov. He scored the try.'

Bloody Sterling. There I was, doing my best, having the time of my life, and he gave me up, ruining my 14 minutes of make-believe.

And then, of course, there was the famous try in the

1992 Grand Final, the decider of my first season back in the fold. The Brisbane Broncos were playing St George at the Sydney Football Stadium, and the ball went out to Steve Renouf in the centres.

Well, he was Ren-oof when he got the ball, Ren-off as he ran 20 metres down the field, back to Ren-oof at the halfway line, and when he scored the try he was Ren-off again. I was totally put off by Sterling, who was sowing the seeds. He always tries to implant the wrong idea in my mind.

Billy Birmingham, better known as the 12th Man, immortalised this call on one of his CDs: 'If you run off Ren-off often enough, you'll score tries!' Hilarious!

When you look at Fatty and Sterlo, one thing comes to mind: you don't have to be all that handsome to get your head on TV. Sterling, in particular. If ever there's a remake of *ET* or *Gandhi*, he'll be a leading candidate to get a start.

I always felt very sorry for the make-up girl at Channel Nine. Can you imagine having only a matter of seconds to make Sterling and Vautin presentable? Sterling would need zero time on hair, but an hour – minimum – for the rest.

Their nicknames tell the story so well: 'the Fat' and 'Snorkeller'. In Vautin's words, 'That will do me.'

I mentioned Ian Frykberg in this chapter. In March of

2014 he passed away. Ian gave me my second chance in this business, and I will never forget his friendship and belief in me.

Above: The earliest photo of me, back in the mid-1940s.

Above right: With my eldest sister Gwen, who was like a second mother to me. Sadly, she passed away late in 2013.

Below: My childhood home in Junee. Mum always wanted me to go to Sunday School but I thought the journey was too far!

Left: Me at 14 years old, with my father, Joe, and brother Bob, who was 19.

Opposite top: Winning the best and fairest award while playing Aussie rules for Junee, with my dad looking on.

Opposite below: My first wife, Monica, and I moved to Canberra, where I began my career as a police officer. From left: Mum, Monica, me and the Police Commissioner.

At the racetrack, where I got the chance to broadcast with my hero, Ken Howard. With us is his understudy, John Tapp, a great mate of mine. In many ways, this was the realisation of my dream.

Opposite: At the 2GB card table for a rugby league match in the early 1970s.

Above: With Ron Casey while
working for 2GB.

Opposite top: Calling a match
with Rex Mossop in the 1970s.

Opposite below: A gathering
of sports commentators: from
left, Alan Marks (ABC), Doug
Melton (2KY), Ray Warren
(2GB), the restauranteur, Frank
Hyde (2SM), Tiger Black (2KY),
Ron Casey (Channel 9), John
O'Reilly (ABC), Geoff Prenter
(2UE) and Col Pearce (2UE).

With tennis legend and my occasional co-commentator John Newcombe – a great friend.

Right: With rugby league identity Peter Wynn and champion jockey Malcolm Johnston.

Below: With my brothers and sisters at my brother Jack's 50th wedding anniversary party. *Back row from left*: Ray, Jack and Bob; *front row from left*: Val, Betty, Gwen and June.

Opposite top: The jumper of which I am most proud. When I started working for Channel Nine, I bought a jumper and sewed on the Nine logo myself.

Opposite below: With the renowned supercoach – and one-time co-commentator – Jack Gibson (a great thrill).

Above: With champion boxer 'Aussie Joe' Bugner. I actually called some boxing with Joe. Great bloke!

Cher and me on our wedding day (*above left*), and with my dad and my son Chris (*above right*).

Right: My young bloke Mark gets a break, calling the schoolboys' Commonwealth Bank Cup final for Channel Nine. Is he coming to get me? Maybe I need a haircut!

Left: My parents, Joe and Win Warren, celebrating 65 years of marriage in 1988. Mum passed away not long after.

Below: With my Channel Nine colleagues Steve Roach, Paul Vautin and Peter Sterling at my 50th birthday celebrations.

Above: The statue of me in my home town of Junee. As a family, we are so proud of this. (Photo courtesy of Declan Rurenga of the Junee *Southern Cross*)

Right: With my mother-in-law, Eve, a great character but a hopeless punter!

Opposite top: On the beach with my beautiful daughter Holly – looks like a profound conversation.

Opposite below: With my sons Mark and Chris (*left*) and with Holly on her 16th birthday (*right*).

Giaan Rooney, Duncan Armstrong and me calling the swimming, along with my lovely, loyal and ever-helpful mate, Adam Harvey, who sadly passed away in 2010.

With my four wonderful grandkids, Matilda, Bobby, Fred and Joe.

15

DEAFIE

We've all heard about the colourful characters who surround racing; I mentioned a few a little earlier in this book. It really is one of the most interesting sports. Some of the best nicknames and some of the most devious people in the world all come together in this sporting capsule that is called the racetrack.

In Sydney we had many. There was the guy known as 'Tube of Blood' – a great nickname. He was so thin, like a pretzel, and wore a gabardine coat all the time. Then there was 'Curly the Caterpillar' – God knows where that came from. Like the Tube of Blood, he didn't have much of an impact but his name was great. There was 'Lemonade Tom', 'Hoppy Bob' and many, many more.

Then there was George Freeman.

One day a mate of mine, Judda, introduced us. I had met Judda at a casino in Rozelle, and he asked me if I'd like to play a round of golf. 'Sure,' I said. 'I'll bring a mate, and you do the same.'

The venue was the Oatlands Golf Club. I brought along the professional from the Cumberland Golf Club, John Ruggiero. I might have said to Ruggs, as we called him, not to mention that he was a pro . . . It might give us an edge, I thought, just a little one. When you're playing blokes you don't really know, sometimes they can inflate their handicaps.

We met at the course. Judda had brought a friend who was smallish, well-tanned and with snow-white hair. He introduced him as George. We had no idea who he was.

Halfway through the round Ruggs and I were winning easily, and I bought lunch for everyone. A few sandwiches and cups of tea later, I had spent around $20. Then we resumed the game. After 18 holes Ruggs and I were up about $300 — and Ruggs had played off scratch, by the way.

Next Judda suggested a game of cards. 'Sure,' I said, knowing full well that Judda spent most of his time at the casino. He suggested euchre, and it was on. Three hours later

Ruggs and I had not only lost the $300 we were ahead, but we'd lost another $300 as well.

It was now settling time, and Ruggs had turned pale white. 'I haven't got the cash on me,' he whispered to me. 'Not $300, anyway.' Nor did I.

I looked at George and Judda and suggested I would pay Judda the outstanding amount the next weekend, at the casino.

At that, George spoke up. 'No worries, Rabs,' he said. 'You bought lunch so let's call it quits. We've had a good day, haven't we, and we didn't come here to hurt each other.'

I was stunned – I'd spent $20 on lunch and owed him $300, and he was suggesting we should call it quits? Apologetically, but also with a little guilt, having brought my pro golfer friend with me, I said: 'That is nice of you, George, but we really must pay.'

'Don't be silly,' he said. 'It's been a fun day and I have to make tracks. I'll see you round the traps.'

A day or so later I rang Judda. 'Mate, who the bloody hell was that bloke George?'

'Rabs, that was George Freeman, you idiot! I thought you knew him.'

Of course I had heard of George Freeman, who had a reputation for fixing races and benefiting from 'other interests'.

At the track I had often heard blokes say, 'You'd better be on this horse – Freeman has backed it,' and things like that. But I'd had no idea that this little bloke was him! Anyway, the George I met on the golf course and over the card table was okay to me and my mate – for at least 300 good reasons!

The other bloke who came from a similar category of 'colourful racing identities' was Bob Trimbole. I don't know if they actually ever pinned anything on 'Aussie Bob', as he was known, but he seemed to roam as free as a bird from track to track with no restrictions.

One day at Gosford, a mate of his introduced us. Bob was as bald as a badger. Well, not quite – he had two strips going along the sides of the bald patch on top. You know the look. Anyway, that night, as we always did, my mates and I went to Claude Fay's Hotel at Hornsby for a drink before getting into our cars for the trip home. It was a good pub.

There we were, having a quiet one, when this same bloke came and introduced us to his mate, Bob Trimbole, again. But now Bob had put a wig on. As a rug, it looked okay, and the difference it made to his appearance was unbelievable.

There is no way the bloke at the races and the bloke in the pub standing next to me are the same person, I thought. But it was! It was Trimbole. The bloke whose name was, rightly or wrongly, linked to drugs, murders, you name it.

One day someone said to me they were looking for Trimbole in relation to a crime. My immediate reaction was: 'Well, good luck, just know that if he's wearing his wig, he looks totally different. Tracking him down will be nigh on impossible.'

They say Aussie Bob is now dead and buried. But it seemed to me there were two Bob Trimboles, his disguise was so complete, so whether they buried the right one, I'm not sure! I met a bloke who was at his funeral and reckoned he was definitely six feet under. 'I'll take twos on,' he told me. 'I saw them bury him.' Maybe so, but I'm still not sure.

But of all the colourful racing identities, both in and beyond the media, Kenny Callander – the racing journalist and tipster for News Limited, and formerly the 'Wizard of Odds' for Channel Nine – remains my favourite.

First of all, he's my mate. Then he's a confidant. Then he's excellent company. Then he's so loyal and so sincere. I don't live in his pocket, and I don't need to. But I do know that when I need advice, Ken is one of the first people I will ring.

He's also the reason why it's taken me so long to write a book.

'Why don't you write a book?' someone asked me a few years ago.

'There's no need to,' I replied. 'Just buy Ken Callander's book and you've read my book. He's filled half his book up with my stories.' Unfortunately, most of them are true!

Deafie and I have had many good times, although I still say not enough. His trademark story about me is from the blackjack table in Brisbane one night. In his book he embellishes the story beyond belief, saying I had $1200 on the turn of a card. He must have confused me with Kerry Packer!

The truth of the matter was that Sterlo, Deafie and I were at the Treasury Casino. We'd had a few ales and a good night – well, Sterlo and Deafie had, and so they'd retired to the bar. I was losing so I continued at the table. My funds dwindled away, so I bit Deafie for a loan.

I was down to my last, so I went with whatever was in front of me. The dealer gave me ten – wow, here we go!

Then I got a two – shit. I took a card – a nine – and blew up big-time, profanity followed by profanity; I was raucous to the point of being embarrassing.

Out of the blue, I heard Deafie yelling out like only he could – 'You little beauty, Rabs!' – and then he was slapping me on the back.

'What are you talking about, you fool?' I said.

'You've got 21,' he cried out. 'He can't beat you!'

'You idiot,' I said. 'Twelve and nine is 22 – I've busted! That's what I'm blowing up about.'

'Rabbies, you're the idiot,' Deafie carried on. 'You are a prize mathematical idiot. You have 21! Pick up your money and let's get out of here.'

I felt exactly like the idiot he had called me, as I muttered my apologies to the dealer and snuck off in the direction of the bar.

I'll never forget going to Deafie's send-off from the racing newspaper *The Sportsman* in 1977. The paper put on a big party in Chinatown. I went along with a mate from the press called Billy George. We went in my car, and the function was just a stone's throw from 2GB, where I worked at the time. I said to Bill, 'I'll park up this blind alley. We'll be okay here, and it's close to where we're going.'

The night passed, with lots of fun, lots of gags and plenty of gee-ups. Finally, it was time to go, and Bill and I made our way back to the alley. 'You drive,' I said. 'I'll stop the traffic in Sussex Street while you back out.'

What Bill didn't know was that I'd been in the police force in another life, and so I'd learnt the fine art of directing traffic. There I was, directing traffic in Sussex Street, in the middle of the city, in the middle of a busy Friday night.

I ordered one car to stop, and suddenly all four doors flew open. Four men dressed in suits got out, flashed their police badges and frog-marched me to their car, telling me I was under arrest for obstructing traffic.

They took me to Central Police Station. The desk sergeant wanted to throw me in the cells. According to Deafie's version of the story, I replied: 'You can't throw me in there with that lot, I call the Amco Cup!'

I don't recall saying that, but even if I did it didn't have any effect, and in I went. There I was with 20 or 30 blokes who were obviously full-time drunks or felons or both. The smell was not nice, there was one toilet between all of us, and they threw me a blanket and a pillow. I was in prison! Chopper, Darcy and Rabs – can you imagine?

As Deafie told the story, Billy had to ring my wife. 'Leave

him there,' she told him. 'It will teach him a lesson.'

I'd certainly made a goose of myself, but I'm sure Monica wasn't that unforgiving.

They could have bailed me, but instead they decided to leave me. When the cops woke me up at five in the morning to tell me I could leave, I was so disappointed. It was the best sleep I'd ever had!

'Out,' one of the coppers said.

And out I went, straight to Central Station to catch the train home to Seven Hills and my always sympathetic wife. In truth, it was one of the most embarrassing moments of my life, but you know, I learnt something about another walk of life. I'm not sure what it is, but let's say they were different.

One of the funniest and strangest nights of my life was alongside Deafie, and it involved the man I was intimidated by more than anyone else, including Jack Gibson and Ron Massey: Kerry Packer.

Big KP. If I saw him coming, I'd get lost, and pretty quickly. Scared? Probably not. Intimidated? Absolutely. I was intimidated by his mere presence. He would sometimes come around the outside broadcast trucks before a match at the Sydney Football Stadium, and as soon as I spied him I'd vamoose.

In 1999 an invite arrived in the mail, inviting Cher and me to the wedding of Kerry's son, James, to his fiancée, the model Jodhi Meares.

'How good is this?' said Cher, excited.

'I don't want to go,' I blurted straight out. 'I've never had to confront Kerry and I don't want to.'

'You're kidding,' she said. 'This is going to be one of the great nights!'

In the end she convinced me to go. A limousine picked us up out the front of our home in Castle Hill, and took us to the Packer compound at Bellevue Hill, in Sydney's eastern suburbs.

It was flogging down rain and there was a long queue of limousines. When we made it to the front of the queue, James, Jodhi, Kerry and his wife, Ros, were welcoming everybody. They were all standing in the atrium as we got out of the car. I was absolutely shitting myself about meeting Kerry. *How am I going to dodge him?*

I told Jodhi she looked lovely, then I thanked James for inviting us. Then we got to Ros.

'Mrs Packer, thanks for the invite. I'm Ray Warren,' I told her.

'Yes, Ray, I know who you are,' she laughed, before turning to my wife. 'You must be Cher?'

Wow, I thought. *She knows my wife's name!* They started a long conversation.

The queue was pushing us forward again, and we came to Kerry Packer, the richest man in the country, who also happened to own Channel Nine. He held out his massive hand; it was like shaking hands with a titan.

'Thanks for the invite, Mr Packer,' I said nervously.

He didn't answer. He just shook my hand, but he was looking at Ros, not me. 'Ros, you can't talk to everybody,' he said angrily. 'They're all getting fucking drowned out there, waiting to get in.' He then pushed me on.

It was the most insincere handshake you'll ever have. I felt like I was a sheep that had just been shorn and shoved down the ramp, into the pen. I sort of got pushed under his armpit.

There were a lot of people there, but Cher and I would spend much of the night with Kenny Callander and his wife, Helen. Very early in proceedings, I said to Deafie: 'Whatever we do, we can't make fools of ourselves in front of Packer. I'm worried we'll do that at some stage tonight.'

This was going to be some event. Eddie McGuire was the master of ceremonies. B.B. King, Human Nature and Elton John were all due to perform. They moved us into a large lounge area, where they were going to handle the speeches. If you couldn't get a seat, there were cushions spread around the floor. So there was me, Deafie, Cher and Helen Callander, sitting there like four chimpanzees, watching what was going on.

I had a bad hip and shoulder on my right-hand side in those days, and they were both giving me curry. The cushions we were sitting on were the worst things for my dodgy hip. I tried to tell Deafie this but he couldn't hear me.

Then, halfway through James's speech, Ken let out: 'Ooh!'

'Keep the noise down, you prick,' I whispered to him.

'I've got a cramp! I've got a cramp!'

He grabbed me by my sore shoulder and leant over to get some support, in the process knocking me sideways off my cushion. Then it was a domino effect, and Cher, then Helen, crashed arse over head.

I was the last to get up. As I rose, I took a glance behind us, and who do you think was there? Kerry Packer . . . and the prime minister, John Howard.

That wedding was the only time I ever actually met

Mr Packer. What an introduction. I did have one other encounter with him, though. I was the MC at a function, and in passing I made the comment that I loved my job so much that I would do it for nothing.

A big, booming voice came from the back of the room: 'Well, if that's the case, why not give me the money back and we'll start again!'

It was Packer!

Later in life, I became friends with John Cornell, who was instrumental in the rise of World Series Cricket alongside Kerry. I told John that Kerry had always intimidated me.

'He liked you a lot, you know?' he told me.

For all those years, I'd been dodging him, when he actually liked me!

Another very funny story about Packer relates to Darrell Eastlake. Mr Packer half-owned an outstanding horse called Easter. The owner of the other half was its trainer, the legendary Tommy Smith.

Eastlake was working at Nine one night, and the horse had just raced that day. The phone rang. It was Packer. 'I'm ringing to see how Easter went,' he said.

'Good,' Darrell said. 'We went up to Nelson Bay. Had a great time.'

'Not *your* Easter, *my* Easter!'

'Well, how's your Easter gone, Mr Packer?' Darrell enquired politely.

By now, KP was enraged. 'Not my Easter, not your Easter, MY BLOODY EASTER! How did it go?'

Big D put his hand over the mouthpiece and turned to Ken Sutcliffe. 'He wants to know how Easter went, Kenny. What the hell is he talking about?'

'It's his horse,' Sutcliffe said. 'Tell him it ran third and it was a good run.'

'Mr Packer, it ran third and it was a good run,' Darrell said into the phone.

'Good,' Packer said. 'Who the hell am I talking to here?'

'Ken Sutcliffe, Mr Packer,' Darrell said. 'Have a nice evening!'

Only Ita Buttrose and Ron Casey can rival Ken Callander's famous lisp. And even they don't quite equal him. I've spoken to Ita and I've worked with Casey, but I never got the shower from them as I do from Ken. 'Sunshine Sue and Sunshine Sammy, and you should back number six in race seven . . . It's got some sort of chance in this race at Sandown . . . Sure, it's the son of Star System, but still there's a heap of hope of it showing speed sufficient enough to secure to shallots . . .'

For God's sake, someone pass the face washer and a poncho!

16

GUS

The match was in Melbourne, but we had entered
Planet Gus back in Sydney, at the airport.

When I arrived at Mascot to take a flight south
for a Melbourne Storm match a few years ago, he didn't say
hello. He didn't speak at all. He didn't even grunt. He just
sat there, like a dugong: a big, immovable object, slowly
opening his eyes as he sent a text. He just texted and texted
and texted. To whom, I don't know, and I don't really care.

Don't get me wrong: I love the man. But if Gus has got
any problem, it's that the game of rugby league consumes
him. This exhausts not only him but also those of us around
him. And that's why, when we're taking a flight together, I
usually go straight to the counter before we board and ask,

'Which seat is Mr Gould in?' And if I'm sitting next to him, I ask to change.

If I'm sitting next to Gus, I know I'm in for an hour and a half of rugby league talk. The game is not ingrained in me, as it is in him. Andrew Voss was the same when he worked at Nine. If you sat next to him, he just talked football. That's why he and Gus made a wonderful pair.

I don't much like sitting next to Peter Sterling, either, because he always suggests the plane we're on is making a peculiar noise and something is wrong and it's going to crash. Either that or he goes to sleep and I've got nobody to talk to.

I think Gus likes sitting next to me, because he knows he aggravates me. But when we caught this particular plane to Melbourne, it didn't matter. He hadn't spoken a word, so I just thought, *Oh well, he's in one of those moods. He's in his own world.*

When we arrived at Melbourne Airport, he shadowed me. He usually follows me around like a sheep dog, because he knows I will have organised the trip perfectly. I like to plan my trips. I like to know if we're getting a hire car or being picked up, and, if we are, where the limo will be.

So we got in the limo. I jumped in the front, he jumped in the back. Then, all of a sudden, he started to sing. He'd sing a verse, then whistle the next. I can't remember the tune, but I can tell you Gus can't sing, nor can he whistle.

'I love travelling with Rabbits,' he cheerily told the driver. 'We get to ride in a limo.'

Do you really think the driver cares? I thought. *He doesn't even know who either of us is!*

I turned around and looked at him. 'Which one are you now?' I asked.

'What do you mean?' he asked. 'What are you talking about?'

Welcome to Planet Gus!

When we go to matches in Melbourne, we usually stay at the Hilton on the Park so we can walk down past the MCG to AAMI Park.

'What time are we leaving for the ground?' Gus will ask me after we check in.

'Well, I'm going down about a quarter past six,' I tell him.

'Alright, I'll walk with you.'

So we'll take that 15-minute walk around the MCG to AAMI Park, and he won't say another word. He'll become another Gus. And I'll wonder to myself: *Why did he want to walk with me if he doesn't want to say a word?*

When we arrive and sit down for the football match, out

will come the chips and the pie. Then the bottle of Coke. And then, at about the seven-minute mark of the match, he will finally have something to say. And it will always, without fail, be something brilliant and insightful.

The day I turned 60, we were calling a game in Brisbane, at Suncorp Stadium. I walked into the commentary box and Louise Macri, our assistant producer, said, 'Happy birthday, Rabs.' Matthew Johns was there that night, and he too said, 'Happy birthday, Rabs.' Now, Matty's got a fairly loud voice so it would've been very audible. Then the executive producer of league at Nine – and Deafie's son – Matthew Callander said, 'Happy birthday, Rabs.'

Not Gus. He just was sitting and texting, at the front of the commentary box, well within earshot of all these people. He still hasn't wished me a happy birthday, and that was ten years ago! I turned 70 last year and I still haven't heard from him.

But as I said, I love him . . . the weirdo that he is!

★

The wise decision to bring Gus into the Nine commentary box was made by Gary Burns, the former head of sport.

As an analyst, Gus is just a freak. He can convert what he's thinking into words, and do it quickly – and that is gold in broadcasting. He took to television commentary so well, and he really understands what he's doing.

I'm not forgetting Peter Sterling in any of this. Sterlo also went from football to commentating brilliantly. They both have their specialities. Sterling has the ability to know when a player should kick; which option is good or bad. I might be thinking, *That's a really good kick*, but Sterlo will be looking through a finer set of glasses. A halfback's set of glasses. He's got a wealth of knowledge.

But Gus comes up with so many different things about the game, things I could never have thought of. That's why I'm happy to sit back and let him and Sterlo do their thing. All I try to do is make it a bit more exciting for the viewer.

What Gus has – more than any other commentator or football brain I have ever seen – is the ability to 'first-guess'. Most people can only second-guess, or analyse what has happened after the event. But Gus seems to know what's going to happen.

We might go to the half-time break with the Knights leading 14–4, and he'll say, 'I wouldn't mind having something on the Roosters. They're ten behind but I think they can come over the top of this mob.' And then, of course, the Roosters will score in the final ten minutes and win. Maybe it is just Gus gambling – I don't know, but he's very often right.

Gus has also got a flair for entertainment, even if he knows he's labouring the point. Every Sunday afternoon, when the sun's shining, I know I am going to hear it: 'Rabbits, Sunday afternoon,' he'll say, slowly and in a deep voice. 'Look at them on the hill. Is there anything better in life than Sunday afternoon at the football?'

He says it every time. And now it's become an entertainment in itself: how long into the match will it be before Gus says he loves Sunday afternoon footy?

I have always been of the view that the bottom line of what we do is entertainment. There are many ingredients to the performance: knowledge of the game; the ability to forecast what's going to happen; the technicalities of the sport; the injection of some humour. If we leave any one of those ingredients out of our performance, then I don't think we're performing to our best.

Remember the night Gus threatened to jump out the window in Newcastle if the video referees gave a controversial try to the Dragons? And then they did? Matty Johns was the sideline commentator, and stood down there with his arms wide open, ready to catch Gus. Those listening on SportsEars stood as one and said, 'So jump!'

All Gus's other classic lines live long in my memory. 'No! No! No! No! No!' I can't remember when he first said that, or how many times he's said it since, but I love hearing it. 'Wow! Get that into ya! Get out of my road, Rabbits!'

He also likes to ask me things directly: 'What's that penalty for, Rabbits?' *I don't know what it's for, Gus!* I'll think. *I'm trying to call the game! Leave me alone!*

I remember the night at AAMI Park during the finals in 2013, when the Knights upset the Storm. We had great fun with the seagulls that were on the field. Our running conversation about those seagulls took up half the game! Gus couldn't work out why this one lone seagull was up the other end on its own. He made the bloody seagulls more important than Smith, Slater and Cronk.

Do I ever fear we labour this stuff too much? Oh, shit yes. But that's the gamble. These squabbles probably fit under the heading of humour. They certainly fit under the heading of entertainment. Whether you like it or not, those funny moments are easily the highlight of Gus's week.

I actually go away on holidays with Gus, and we've never had a genuine blue. We sometimes have a difference of opinion, sure. He picks on referees, while I believe they're only doing what's in the book. If you don't like the rule, then change the rulebook. But the bottom line is we're trying to entertain. That's what it's all about.

If Gus has got a problem, it's that the public don't understand him. They don't know him. Much of that is because of how he's treated by certain sections of the press. That hurts *me*. I don't know how much of it he deserves, because we all get a bit of that. Every single one of us in the media who gets a bit of criticism asks ourselves if we deserve it. In Gus's case, he works for a television network and a newspaper, and the opponents of those two institutions give it to him. That's the game. You've got to be prepared for some flak.

Yet it worries me that people get the wrong impression of Gus because of the little turf wars that go on in the media, but which not everyone is aware of. There are vendettas and there are rivalries between certain individuals, and now people use the keyboard to vent their spleen in gossip columns.

I don't think it really hurts Gus. At least, he doesn't show it outwardly. I can say for sure that I've never seen it faze him. I've walked into the commentary box on some days and said, 'Jesus, you've copped it big this morning in the Sunday newspaper.' And he doesn't even respond. He just stares out at the ground, then gets his phone out and sends another text to Nick Politis. I guess it's Nick, anyway.

Gus is a genius at the text. I have trouble sending a message to my wife to tell her I love her. Not Gus. In the middle of a match, he'll know what's trending on Twitter, and what the scores are at the other grounds. Nick will be on a Greek island and Gus will be giving him a running commentary of the game. He can do five things at the same time. He's obsessive – about the game and about everything else he does.

I'm not like that. Some time ago, when my contract was up for renewal, I told Nine's head of sport, Steve Crawley, Matt Callander and Brad McNamara – the former NSW cricketer who is now the executive producer of cricket – that I wanted more time off. 'Look, I'm just starting to feel like I need some more time at the weekends with my daughter,' I said.

'Well, just work whatever Sundays you want to work,' they said.

So I started taking almost every second Sunday off. One

Sunday, I was out the back mowing the grass, and my phone rang. It was David Gyngell, the chief executive of Nine. 'Where the bloody hell are you?' he barked.

'I'm mowing the lawn,' I said.

'Mowing the lawn? Don't you realise there's a war on?'

'What war?' I said, wondering where this was going. 'What are you talking about?'

'We're in a ratings war,' David said. 'And Sunday night is important. The Sunday news is the foundation, and it gets its foundation from the football. And the head caller is mowing the lawn?'

'Well, fair enough,' I said. 'I'll work more Sundays then.'

Little did I know that the other scallywags hadn't told Gyngell about the Sundays off that they'd given me. 'You really got me into big trouble, you lot,' I told them the next Sunday, at the footy. I used more colourful language than that, but you get the drift.

During this time, Gus was complaining about my absence. 'I wouldn't mind getting some time off myself, you know?' he said more than once. 'It always seems to be Rabs getting time off, and I get nothing.'

So the next time Matt Callander did the rosters, he gave Gus the Sunday off. The only problem for Gus was that, as it happened, our match that week was at Cronulla, right near where he lives. He blew up like a toad at being given a day off when there was a match on at Cronulla. So what do you think he did? He went to the football anyway and sat right in front of the commentary box.

Gus just can't keep away from the game, and, as I've said, it exhausts him. Most of the time, Gus has an enormous and insatiable desire to work. But occasionally he'll say, 'I'm sick of this. This'll do me.' Then five minutes later he'll ask if there's any more work for him.

In May 2011, when he accepted the position as general manager at the Penrith Panthers, I gave him a sermon about doing too much work. 'You're writing for Fairfax, you're working for Nine – why do you want to take on this job too?' Not only has he turned the club around and put it on the right path, but he's also given it a future. He's taken on the expansionist AFL in the western suburbs of Sydney, and the jury is out on that.

Despite all his other interests, I'm sure that the 80 minutes on a Sunday afternoon are his favourite 80 minutes of the week. Everyone knows he's right about Sunday footy. It's a shame we are abandoning daytime footy. TV's been good to me, but the gradual disappearance of daytime footy is a downside to TV's involvement in the game. Night-time footy just draws bigger ratings.

Even though I know Gus is right about it, I don't think I'm as passionate as him when it comes to afternoon footy. That would be impossible. But when it ends for me, I'll certainly miss being there with him.

You get different values in life as you get older. But I know one thing: it's never dull on Planet Gus.

17

THE VOICE

I think I've been a better broadcaster in the latter part of my life, particularly since I joined Nine. My voice has also changed – I hope for the better!

People talk about my voice a lot. They tell me I sound like a bloke who's drunk a bottle of scotch and smoked a packet of Winfields every day of his life. Now, that's just not correct . . . at least, it's not correct now. I jest, although I was once a heavy smoker and I did like a whiskey.

I never drink or have drunk on game day, or during a match. But I did like a cigarette, particularly 'OPs' – other people's. In the 1990s I would smoke a packet of cigarettes during the course of the morning program I once hosted on the radio station 2KY. I'd knock off a packet in three hours, no worries. When I was at Ten, I was smoking and calling and smoking and calling. When I started at Nine, Sterling and Vautin blew up big-time that I was puffing away in the broadcast box, so I had to give it away.

That was actually the second time I gave the wretched things the flick. In the early 1980s I saw the well-known ear, nose and throat specialist Dr John Tonkin, who once operated on the former NSW premier Neville Wran. He examined me at his surgery in Macquarie Street in the city, and the prognosis was grim.

'I want you to go to St Vincent's Hospital straight away, and I'll operate first thing tomorrow,' he said. 'You've got nodules on your vocal cords.'

That frightened the hell out of me and I went straight to St Vincent's – or the Darlinghurst Hilton, as it was sometimes known. Someone from Ten sent me a slab of Victoria Bitter and I ended up having a few beers with one of the nurses. I wasn't smoking, though.

Dr Tonkin operated, and when I woke up he told me that he'd removed the nodules and had sent them away for testing. He was almost certain they would be benign, but it was a nervous wait nonetheless.

'If you don't stop smoking,' he said, 'you won't be living

this dream you've been talking about for much longer.'

He didn't explicitly say I was going to die, but he made it very clear that my voice would. The tests showed that the nodules weren't cancerous. I eventually gave up the fags.

When I listen to recordings of my voice in the 1970s and 1980s, it's obvious to me that the nodules were interfering with how it sounded. When I was free of them, my voice changed quite dramatically, becoming what it is today.

I had no voice training to speak of. In my early days, I was trying to sound like someone else, then I finally realised it was best to sound like myself. It was easier that way. And now people are impersonating me. It doesn't get more humbling than that.

'Look, I've just been given some inside mail on some changes to this New Zealand rugby league side for the Tri-Nations final . . . The hooker is Varicos Vain-o-colo. The props: Willie Tell-lou-a-lie and He'll-only-ever-light-a-lou. The second-rowers: In-early-had-a-nookie and If-she-only-found-my-weiner. The lock is Lighten Up-a-bunger. The halfback is St– St– St– Bloody tongue-twister! Stacey Jones.'

Just to clarify, that's not me but Billy Birmingham, the

man of a thousand voices who has made a living mimicking every Australian sports broadcaster worth his salt over the last three decades on his very funny 12th Man albums. He started off with Richie Benaud and Bill Lawry and Tony Greig from Nine's star-studded cricket commentary team, and then a few years back he turned his attention to me. His rendition of me going through the New Zealand Test team has become a classic.

We've spent many hours together, talking sport and other gibber, on *Dead Set Legends* on Triple M in Sydney most Saturday mornings. Billy tells me that I'm the most impersonated person in Australia, alongside Richie Benaud. I don't know whether that's a good thing or not. I believe I was elevated after John Howard lost the prime ministership in 2007. I shot up in the rankings then. Thanks, Johnny.

Anyway, Billy has got many miles out of me. One day when I was on the *Legends* and he had a day off, he phoned in. 'Reg Warren here,' he said, doing me. 'Can I speak to Rabbits?'

'Yes, who are you?'

'It's your brother Reg, Ray,' said Billy. 'I'm still in Junee. I'm the one you don't want to recognise. I was the black sheep of the Warren family, wasn't I, Ray?'

'Billy, you know there's no Reg.'

'I'm still in Junee calling the dogs, Ray.'

It was hilarious stuff – Billy prodding, me defending, knowing all along it was him and he was just having some fun at my expense. Little did I realise it would irritate my brother Jack to the extent that it did.

Jack was 86 and listening to the show. He had never heard of Billy, so he got on the phone to me straight after I left the studio.

'Who's this Reg Warren?' he demanded. 'We don't have another brother. Who is this idiot? It's a bloody insult!'

'Jack, Jack, Jack,' I said. 'Hold your horses. It's a comedian impersonator mate of mine taking the piss. It's all a joke.'

'Well, I don't care about him taking the piss and I don't like his jokes – it's a bloody insult! There is no other brother. How could he say we concealed some other brother or sister or whatever?'

Jack was in a serious lather and I told him I'd ask Billy to lay off. Now, however, he listens to the 12th Man and loves it!

For many, many years – for much of my career, to be honest – I was embarrassed and angry when I heard someone mimicking my voice. There was a time in Lismore, after I'd called an Amco Cup match involving Balmain, when I was standing in the corner of the saloon bar of a local hotel.

Tigers half back Ronnie Ryan and one of their forwards, John Elias, were in the other. I could hear them chirping away at me from across the room, so I walked over and confronted them. They weren't calling me names, they were just doing my voice. It was the first time it had happened.

'You blokes got a problem, have you?' I asked.

I didn't offer to take it outside, and I'm glad I didn't. I could've handled Ronnie. He's become a good friend since. He does my voice better than I do it myself, although he's a pest. He'll ring and leave a message on my mobile phone at 3 am, doing my voice. He's a good kid.

All these years later – and it's about three decades since that night – I'm flattered when I hear people impersonating me. Plenty of people do a great impression. My son, Mark, sounds just like me. Dave Gibson on Triple M was good at it during the 1990s. In fact, we had a segment called 'Rabs versus Rabs', where we would both do my voice. And of course there's Billy Birmingham.

I often do interviews across the country around Origin or Grand Final time to promote Nine's coverage, and one of the radio hosts is bound to have a crack. 'Can you listen to this, Rabs?' they will say. 'It's me doing you?'

'Mate,' I usually say, 'I'd stick to playing music.'

And then there are the dozens of people who I see out and about in public. I'll be coming down an escalator at the footy or at a shopping centre, and someone will yell 'Rabby!' And I think, *Here we go . . .*

I used to hate it. Now it makes me proud.

★

I'm often asked which player I loved calling the most. Of course, Steve Menzies was one of them. He scored a lot of tries for Manly, particularly at their home ground, Brookvale Oval, during my early years at Nine. I also had a lot of fun calling Eric Grothe, the bustling and bearded Parramatta winger in the 1970s and 1980s. His iconic try from close range at the SCG, in a semi-final against Canterbury in 1983, was as good as it gets.

'*Look at Grothe. Beats one! Beats two! Look at Grothe! Beats three! Beats four! He's beaten five! Oh, what a try! That's one of the best tries you'll ever see!*'

Then there was that classic Brett Mullins try on that freezing Friday night in Canberra. I used to call his father, Bill, when he played off the wing for the Roosters. I'll probably be calling Bill's grandson soon enough, I reckon. I've called Craig Young at St George, then his son Dean at the same club. There was Wayne Pearce at Balmain, and now his son Mitchell Pearce, the premiership-winning halfback at the Roosters. My god, I feel old when I put it like that!

Mullins was one of my all-time favourites, but my feeling towards Billy Slater is very similar. 'The Slater try' – everyone knows what I'm talking about when I say that. Game two of the 2004 State of Origin series, when the Maroons fullback pounced on a grubber kick behind the line from captain Darren Lockyer, then ran and swerved and chip-kicked to regather and score:

'*Darren Lockyer! He kicks. Slater's picked it up! Was he on-side? Slater! Down the ground. Kicks again! He'll get there! He's over! Billy Slater! He will score one of the great Origin tries!*'

I immediately knew how significant that try was. Any commentator is proud when he can be truly in the moment and identify its greatness. The 'miracle' try for Mark Coyne in 1994, when the ball went through 11 sets of hands before the Maroons scored in the final minute, was another one:

'*Trailing 12–10. Langer, pushing it wide. Walters onward. Now for Carne. Carne joins in. Floats the pass for Renouf. Renouf down the touchline. Beats one! Gets it infield! Hancock gets it on! Queensland are coming back! Darren Smith for Langer! Langer gets it away! Here's the Big Fella! Gets the pass on. Coyne! Coyne!*'

Goes for the corner and gets the try! Queensland! It's a miracle performance! That's not a try, that's a miracle!'

The Big Fella, of course, was Mal Meninga. And as anyone who witnessed that moment will remember, Fatty then screamed, 'Oh, yeah, what about that one, Sterlo!' in the background.

In one recent game, I called something a 'miracle', and shortly afterwards Gus shoved his phone under my nose. A text message read: 'You can't use that word for anybody else.' It was from Mark Coyne, who lives near Gus in Sydney's south.

The more freakish the try, the higher I get. When Roosters winger Daniel Tupou scored from a cross-field kick in the 2013 Grand Final against Manly, this came out of me: *'Tupou! Oh, Daniel Tupou, flying at 39,000 feet, with no turbulence to be found!'*

I never script what I'm going to say. It just comes out of me. I don't see that as any special sort of art. What is artistic, I reckon, is when a sports broadcaster has the ability to ad-lib and patter his or her way out of trouble, so the listener doesn't know they're in trouble. To me, that's pure professionalism: ad-libbing your way out of a mile of shit.

Tackles also get me going. People might hear me say 'Uoo-hew!' That's me emphasising the pain. That's me saying, 'Jesus, that must have hurt!'

No tackle could've hurt more than the one Wally Lewis put on Darrell Williams in a Test between Australia and New Zealand at Mount Smart Stadium in 1989. I actually thought Lewis had killed him that day. It was a savage tackle. Williams went to ground and then King Wally, like a world championship wrestler, jumped on him and squashed him. It was the best tackle you will ever see. It wasn't a John Raper-like tackle, where he grassed him around the ankles. It was ball, ribcage, everything.

I know my excitement levels go off the Richter scale in those situations, but I don't think I've ever gone too far. I've never completely lost it. You have to temper yourself. You have to judge the moment. The Coyne try was simple, because it was off the back of 11 pairs of hands. It was always going to be one of the tries of the century.

For historical purposes, I've got to call any try positively, but the video referee has made things tricky. Like the Decision Review System in cricket, deferring to the video referee really ruins the moment, or at least damages it. When it came into the game, I made a conscious decision that I was still going to call tries as I saw them. If they were later turned down, so be it. If I called them negatively, it would affect my overall performance.

One of the most historic moments in rugby league history, as far as the good people of the Hunter Valley are concerned, came in the final minute of the 1997 Grand Final between their beloved Knights and the Manly Sea Eagles. This was the decider of the Australian Rugby League, in a season when the Super League war had split the game in half: Rupert Murdoch's News Limited wanted to seize control and form a rebel league.

I've never before come out and declared my feeling publicly, but I believed what Super League represented was wrong. I had great reservations about the manner in which that whole episode went on.

I could understand what Mr Murdoch wanted to do. He wanted a slice of this major winter sport so he could sell pay TV subscriptions. I was totally aware of that. And he was right in many ways, because Kerry Packer had done the same thing with World Series Cricket in the 1970s. But I wasn't associated with that era at Nine.

People were encouraged to break contracts, and I've always felt strongly about that. My ethics are you don't break a contract unless there's a really good reason and both parties agree. Murdoch's reason was to sell pay TV subscriptions, and in my view that wasn't reason enough to be encouraging young men to break their contracts.

When Nine agreed to show Super League matches that year, I just stood there, shook my head and did my job. But I don't think they ever had the same feeling as the ARL games. So when Knights halfback Andrew Johns skirted down the blind side with a minute to go, then found his winger Darren Albert coming back inside to score the match-winner, you could tell I was happy. *'Albert will score! Albert will score! Newcastle! Has won! The Grand Final!'* Partly, I think, I was happy that this uncomfortable year was finally over.

When Brisbane beat Cronulla in the Super League Grand Final in the same season, I didn't feel the same. I doubt anyone felt good about the year. Put bluntly, it was a bitch of a time.

The question I get asked the most is this: 'How do you do it?' Every sports broadcaster gets the same question. I'll try to explain it as simply as possible.

Let's start with the footy. When I began calling rugby league, I made a point of studying the rules closely. You can't call any sport without knowing the rules, and you've also got to have a good knowledge of the game itself. So if you didn't make first grade as a player, that doesn't bar you from being a caller. Some people who did make the top can't call anyway.

My next priority is to know the players: what they look like, how they run, whether they wear headgear or bandaging. Knowing numbers is only one of many details.

Calling identical twins is strange. The Dawson twins at Newtown many years ago were especially hard. Once, I asked them to wear different coloured tape around their heads. Paul was supposed to wear blue and Chris was supposed to wear white. I think they dudded me once or twice, but from front on it was impossible to tell them apart without it.

Right now, we have the Morris twins, Brett and Josh. A couple of year ago, during a broadcast when they were each playing for Country against City in Mudgee, I said it was nigh on impossible to distinguish between them. Naturally, that attracted some raucous banter from my co-commentators. 'What about their numbers?'

My response was blunt, and said with some delight: 'What if they are running towards me?' The silence was deafening.

The Burgess twins – George and Thomas – are the same, but they wear a different brand of boot. Can you believe that? If you can't see their numbers, that's the only way to distinguish between them.

Easily the most important thing for a sports broadcaster is the ability to ad-lib or patter. This quality, I'm sure, is what separates those who can from those who cannot. If you can patter or ad-lib, you can get through the stickiest of situations. If you can't, you'll stumble and splutter and basically sound stupid or amateurish.

That's more important in racing than in any other sport, I've found. For instance, if there's a horse trapped out wide, beyond the others, you can't see its colours but you know it's there. So do you say, 'There's one out deep, but I can't see its colours . . .'? Or do you cover for a few seconds until you catch a glimpse of it? Believe me, the latter is the way to go, but the ability to do it only comes from experience and confidence.

The greyhounds are another proposition. With them, the biggest hurdle you have to overcome is that they change colours from race to race and week to week. When you call horses, you can study the colours for the races today, and if those same horses come back two weeks down the track, you know they'll be wearing the same colours. But with the dogs, they carry the rug colour according to the box they draw, from one to eight. Memorising their colours is useless. You have to remember them race by race and then get them out of your head. Paul Ambrosoli and Ron Hawkswell are two of the very best at calling the dogs.

Still, we all make mistakes – in any form of broadcasting. Take James Dibble, the ABC newsreader from many years ago. He was reading the news and the autocue broke down. As he fumbled for his papers, he reported: 'A woman at Batemans Bay today was bitten on the funnel by a finger web spider . . .' Not bad for the ABC, I reckon!

Harry Potter, Channel Ten's crime reporter, once famously said: 'A decapitated body was found today in the backyard of a home in Sydney's South, face-down.' A woman on a panel show once said: 'I'd give an arm and a leg to be attractive.'

In sport, though, we make the best bloopers of all. My swimming buddy Nicole Stevenson, the famous backstroker, once told a live television audience that she'd spent the major part of her professional life 'lying on my back and looking at the ceiling'. Wow!

Murray Walker, when calling the Formula One, said: 'The car in front is unique but identical to the car currently in second place.'

A BBC soccer caller, referring to Chelsea striker Julian Dicks, said: 'This Julian Dicks is literally everywhere. It's like there are 11 Dicks on the field.'

Don't get Rex Mossop started on that subject. 'I've got nothing against the male genitalia,' roared the Moose about a beach on the north side of the bridge that was being infiltrated by nudists, 'so long as they don't shove it down my throat.'

I remember a race commentator once said this: 'The Fireman's Ball is getting squeezed against the fence.' Now, that would be painful!

In a race at Mudgee, Ruthless Dick and Cunning Stunt went across the line together. 'It's Dickless Ruth,' said the caller. 'Won by a nose from . . . the other one.'

Manly great Johnny Gibbs once said on *The Footy Show*: 'Take a look at the southern and northern stands. They're not there, but take a look.' He was referring to some demolished stands at Stadium Australia. In more recent times, Brad Fittler was down on the sideline. 'There's a southerly breeze, Rabs, coming out of the south,' he reported. Thanks, Fred. Ben Elias once called a game 'a battle of nutrition'.

I'm not immune from making mistakes. A few seasons ago, I didn't have Storm halfback Cooper Cronk 'chipping' into the corner but 'shitting' into the corner. Oops. And, all these years later, still nobody will forget the very unfortunate slip of the tongue I had with the Broncos fullback Karmichael Hunt.

We all make errors, but that's what happens when you are working on the knife's edge. I used to get the shits with print journos who would pick me up for making a mistake, but I've learnt over the years not to take on anybody in the press. I tell every young caller: 'Don't take on a bloke in the press – he'll beat you every time.'

Print journos have time to correct their mistakes, but the live commentator does not. But even so, the journos still make plenty of grammatical mistakes. I know one reporter in particular who didn't know the different between 'bought' and 'brought'. He got it wrong every time – and he had the audacity to have a crack whenever I got something wrong!

★

I don't write things down in advance, like some commentators do. For me it's about spontaneity – if I write it down, to me it becomes a distraction and always tends to falsify what I am trying to give to the audience.

People often remember when Alan Cann, the chunky Broncos backrower with the big left-foot step, scored a try at the end of a bustling run, and I bellowed, '*Somebody stop him! He'll run out of the stadium!*' That was straight off the top of my head – not that it was so remarkable, but it was spontaneous and reflected my feelings.

There are a lot of sayings in me that I remember from growing up. 'He's showing more toe than a Roman sandal . . . It's as close as a boarding house scrape of butter . . .' I say things like that from time to time and blokes ask, 'Where did you get that from?' And I look at them and think, *Jesus Christ, where have you blokes been?* But that's just me coming from a different era. I reckon Bert Bryant planted some of those sayings in my memory.

I've admired many great callers over the years, in all sorts of sports. Bruce McAvaney is unbelievable. When it comes to athletics, he's without peer. I met him in London on the way home from the Olympic Games in 2012, and that was the first time we'd ever had a decent chat.

Some say that Dennis Cometti, who calls the AFL for Seven, and who has also called swimming for many years, is my equivalent in those parts of the country that don't love rugby league. I've met him only once or twice, but I love listening to him call. He's very silky. Smooth, and with a touch of wit.

I think Tim Lane is very good, as is Peter Donegan, who gets across a lot of different sports. In racing, Greg Miles is the best. And Allan Thomas always captures the moment well in Brisbane. He understands the punter; many don't.

I get asked all the time to name the one match from my commentary career that stands out. I can't – simply because I've done so many. In fact, I couldn't tell you exactly how many games I've called over the years, but a ballpark figure would be around 4000 first-grade league matches, 75 State of Origins, and maybe 100 Test matches. I don't like being away from home, and I hate flying, but once I'm in the commentary box I'm just as passionate as I was when I was sitting at the card table for 2LF or 2GB all those years ago.

And I'm not someone who dwells on the glories of the past and thinks that Noel Kelly or Rex Mossop or whoever were by definition better or tougher than the current crop. If anything, I'm more positive about the current era of players. I look at how Andrew Johns played in the second game of the 2005 Origin series for New South Wales, and I marvel at how he basically did a Wally Lewis in that game, winning it for the Blues. But I can also look back at the 1973 Grand Final, between Manly and Cronulla, and recall what a bloodbath it was before Bob Fulton rose above it.

Sometimes the game's not all that hard to call. Remember when the Bulldogs winger Hazem El Masri had a sideline conversion after the siren against the Knights in 2002? His side was trailing 18–19, and a successful conversion was needed to win it. Only that would silence the big and vocal Newcastle crowd that was roaring at his back.

Such a situation is a caller's dream. I had all the time in the world to enjoy the drama and build it up for the viewers. I don't mean to talk like a chatterbox. It's about knowing when to talk and when not to. Light and shade.

'*Twenty-five thousand people palpitate. The climax to a supreme game of rugby league . . .*'

Pause.

'*El Masri. Trailing by one . . .*'

Pause. You can really feel the tension rising. Drain the moment.

'*This to win it.*'

There's an art to this, and I get shitty when someone wants to butt in. *Shut the hell up*, I think.

'*He's got it away. Look at this! Look at this! Canterbury win on the bell!*'

Two years later, the Bulldogs were celebrating their 70th anniversary. Everyone was dressed up in dinner suits. I was the compere, but I was standing with the audio people beforehand, because I didn't really know too many people there.

Suddenly, an immaculately dressed man came up to me with his wife, who was beautifully clad, wearing a traditional Arab headdress. He put out his hand. 'I'm Hazem El Masri, Ray,' he said.

'Wow,' I replied. I thought he would be smaller than he was. 'I'm used to seeing you in footy gear.'

'I just want to thank you for all the nice things you've said about me over the years.'

That made my cry. That's what makes the job all worthwhile. What a thrill that was. Nobody says thank you much anymore.

18

THE POOL

We are on the blocks at the 2001 Australian Swimming Championships, for the final of the 800-metre freestyle. There are eight men in the race but everyone knows it's between two: the 18-year-old Ian Thorpe and the 1500-metre specialist Grant Hackett. Thorpe is wearing his signature full-length black bodysuit, and he's coming up in distance. The retired Kieren Perkins holds the world record.

'*They should smash the world record,*' I told Channel Nine's viewers. '*Thorpe – the black shark – in lane five, Hackett in four . . .*'

I knew before this race that I was going to get my teeth into it. I was fascinated. After the first 200 metres, I started to have some fun.

'It's almost as though Thorpe is saying to Hackett, "You show me the way. I'm swimming into waters I haven't been in before. I'll follow you and then, if I've got enough petrol, we'll see who's the better man."'

Hackett led for the first half of the race, with Thorpe sitting on his shoulder, as they both settled into their strokes. Now they were approaching the halfway point.

'Now, edging closer, the big, black shark – the Thorpedo – is about to eyeball Hackett . . . Thorpe is getting closer. Hackett in front, still. Grant has got him in his sights. Now they're looking at each other. Thorpe, breathing to his left. Hackett, breathing to his right. "How you going? How you feeling?" That might be the message from Hackett. "I can do this all day. How long can you do it for?"'

My expert commentator, Olympic gold medallist Duncan Armstrong, had predicted before the race that this was where Thorpe would make his move. The camera flashed to Thorpe's pensive coach, Doug Frost, in the stands.

Heading into the final lap, Thorpe took the lead, and suddenly Perkins' world mark was within reach.

'Now Thorpe! Here he comes! He's on his way back! Doug Frost is standing up. Ian Thorpe is blowing Hackett away now.'

He hit the wall.

'There's the world record! There's the world record! He's annihilated that world figure! There is no stopping Ian Thorpe. This is a legend. This is the greatest of all time.'

When it came to the pool, Ian Thorpe was my Billy Slater. My problem with these guys is that I ran out of adjectives. I know that sounds like a cliché, but it's true. That was the only time I wanted to write something down, because I just knew he was going to win – a bit like Greg Miles calling Makybe Diva. From a champion to a legend.

It's amazing, isn't it, how life twists and turns? I used to be too afraid to have a bath, let alone swim. When I was a kid, they would have to throw me into the pool, I was that scared. Little did I suspect that the sport would become such a major part of my career after we had packed away the 1990 Commonwealth Games. Like a bushfire, though, it flared up again during a drink with Gary Burns. It was 1997 and he asked me straight: would I like to go to the 1998 Kuala Lumpur Commonwealth Games?

'Do you want to do the athletics or the swimming?' he asked.

Like the time Ian Frykberg asked me if I wanted to call football on a full-time basis again, it didn't take me long to answer. Athletics is good but our athletes could never do what our swimmers had achieved in Auckland in 1990. Those games were enormously successful for us in the pool, with over 20 gold medals, but it also made Channel Nine aware that this was a sport the people loved. The Dolphins, as the national swim team came to be known, were a ratings magnet.

Sniffing the breeze, Burnsy went after the swimming rights, and secured long-term contracts for all swimming except the Olympics and the Commonwealth Games, which back then belonged to Seven and Ten.

It was swimming that lifted my profile and allowed me to talk to the nation. For the network, the Pan Pacific Championships in Sydney in 1999 continued the swimming ratings bonanza as the network dared to show it during prime-time. It came in at number five or six of the top ten shows of the year across Australia, and we won a Logie for its success. During the 1990s and early 2000s, swimming was in its prime, and we covered it four weeks of the year.

At that time, of course, we were in the middle of the sport's golden age in Australia, with some of the biggest names we've ever seen in the pool. I really wish I had covered

the Sydney Olympics, because Thorpe's swim in the men's
4 x 100-metre relay, when he gave American Gary Hall Jr a
body length heading into the final leg – and that's a bloody
long way – was something special. But earlier that year, at
the Olympic trials in May, I did get to call Susie O'Neill.

'Madame Butterfly', as she was known, was chasing
history: she was attempting to break the world record of
American Mary T. Meagher, set 19 years earlier. It was one
of swimming's longest-standing records. Susie's pursuit of it
became a saga. On this night at the Sydney Aquatic Centre,
Susie went all-out, and the yellow world-record line across
the pool showed how close she was.

'*Susie O'Neill – the vital final lap. She's a length in front.
Petria Thomas is second. It's O'Neill in front. Zero point nine
eight seconds in front of world-record time. There's the line again.
It's wearing her down. O'Neill in front of it! The line is getting her!
O'Neill's in front of it! The line coming at her! Hang on, Susie!
Hang on, Susie! Five to go! You're gonna do it, are you? Susie!
Yes! Yes! Yes! She's done it! A dream has been realised!*'

I never thought I'd be this passionate about swimming.
Never. Here I am now, feeling like I know a bit about the
sport. I can't talk about it like Norman May, who showed me
the ropes at the 1990 Commonwealth Games in Auckland,

but now I feel like I can sit in any company and talk about swimming with confidence.

Swimming reminded me of racecalling, and it gave me a chance to satisfy that yearning for racecalling that I'd had since I was six years old. The swimming community embraced me, because they'd never heard swimming called like I called it. Every race was a Golden Slipper or a Melbourne Cup. It lent itself to that style. There were no colours, just lanes.

At swimming events in those days, the broadcasting area was always open. I had no doubt that those around me were thinking, 'Who is this absolute lunatic?' I'd be at full volume, because we had all these champions: Thorpe, Hackett, Klim, O'Neill, Thomas. It was a beautiful crop.

I also developed a fasciation with Leisel Jones, who had swum at the Sydney Olympics and won silver in the 100-metre breaststroke at the age of just 15. I really built up a liking for her, because she was so young. Gary Burns had also made me aware of the tough circumstances she had faced at home. She was estranged from her father, and her mother, Rosemary, was doing it tough financially. Nine helped her out a bit, inspired by Gary.

At the 1998 Commonwealth Games in Kuala Lumpur, I needed some help, too. As they say, once a gambler, always a gambler. But every so often you run across someone who only bets on a hunch. Such was the case up in Kuala Lumpur. Gerard Daffy, a friend and founder of the corporate bookmaker Centrebet, had been faxing me the betting on the swimming, which I would occasionally mention in the coverage.

Australia had been winning everything, and the prices offered about our swimmers were very short indeed. What was apparent was that if you thought a swimmer from anywhere other than Australia could win, then you'd get incredibly generous odds.

My co-commentators, Duncan Armstrong and Nicole Stevenson, were intrigued by these prices. Betting on the swimming had been unheard of in their day, and for that reason alone it attracted their interest. Well, that was the case until about day five, when one of them asked me to put $200 on a Canadian swimmer, Kelly Stefanyshyn, in the 100-metre backstroke.

I nearly fell over at the size of the bet. 'Let's get the prices first, and then make up your mind,' I told them. 'She might be at huge odds, and you can back her each way, but let's wait until we get the prices.'

The prices came through. Stefanyshyn was 33 to 1.

'For you,' Daffy told me, 'she's 66 to 1.'

'She's 66 to 1,' I told Duncan and Nicole. 'Have $100 each way.'

'No way,' they said. They were adamant they wanted $200 straight out.

'You're mad,' I said again. 'Back her each way.'

'No way.'

I phoned Daffy.

'Okay, mate, we want $13,000 to $200 on Stefanyshyn,' I said.

Daffy nearly swallowed the bloody phone.

'What?!' he said. 'Mate, what's she using? An outboard motor?'

'No, it's just that these two idiots who know nothing about gambling but plenty about swimming want to back this Canadian girl,' I explained.

'Well, mate, you can have the bet this time, but for Christ's sake, we're holding nothing on the race at all and I can't lay off because no one else is working on the swimming,' Daffy said.

I hung up the phone before Daffy had a heart attack or changed his mind. And then I started wondering: who was this Kelly Stefanyshyn? I wanted in.

'Listen,' I told Duncan and Nicole. 'You've only got the 66 to 1 because he thought he was doing me a favour, so can I come in for a third?' They agreed. 'By the way,' I said, 'what are we doing backing her anyway?'

'Well, Meredith Smith is the favourite and she's had some injury problems,' Nicole explained. 'And Giaan Rooney is only a new kid on the block, so there's a good chance the Australians won't win. Besides, Stefanyshyn has a better PB than anyone in the top eight.'

I learnt later in my short career that PB stood for 'personal best'. Coming from an Olympian and 11-time national champion, and supported by an Olympic Gold medallist in Armstrong, it all sounded good.

'Well, this certainly has more logic to it than nine out of ten bets that I would have every day of my life,' I told them.

At the swimming, we use lip-ribbon microphones, like they do at the cricket. You can take them away from your mouth and swear your head off and it won't go to air. They only work when held against your top lip. The 100-metre backstroke doesn't exactly give you much time to get overly excited, but I can tell you, what followed in the next 60 seconds was mayhem.

Smith led early but the other young Aussie, Rooney, down in lane eight, was close up, and Stefanyshyn was back about fourth. With 25 metres to go, Smith was in trouble. Rooney took the lead and the Canadian was coming with a big finish. Normally, you would expect Australian commentators to get excited about an Australian victory, but in this race we gave the distinct impression that the Canadian deserved to win.

Rooney was still in front with ten to go.

'Look at Stefanyshyn!' Nicole screamed.

Who do you think we are looking at, Nicole? I thought. *We're all in this together.*

Armstrong dropped his microphone. 'Go, Kelly!' he screamed.

Now Nicole threw her mic away and they were in unison. 'Go, Kelly!'

I was trying to remain relatively composed. That was hard enough without these two screaming in my ears.

The swimmers hit the wall together. It's close – there's only a touch in it. What takes a split-second seems like an eternity. Have we won $13,000? What a race, what a finish!

Up goes lane eight. It's Giaan!

'Rooney has won it,' I told the viewers. 'It is more gold for Australia.'

'What a wonderful moment for Giaan,' said Duncan.

'Yes, that's the greatest win of the games, good luck to her,' said Nicole.

Forgive us, Giaan. It was $13,000 to us. To you, it was a gold medal, but you now have a mantelpiece full of them. More to the point, Giann, we could have bought you 25 solid-gold medals with our $13,000!

Rooney went on to become the 200-metre freestyle champion of the world. Her courage and desire to win were apparent at all times, but just this once I was wishing silver upon her.

In 2001 we journeyed to Fukuoka in Japan for the World Championships. It was there I saw and called one of the greatest moments in sport I could ever imagine.

Since the retirement of Perkins, Grant Hackett had become the world's leading 1500-metre swimmer. Perkins was great. He was number one, and Australia loved him. But he was superseded, just like footballers are. Hackett was now faster, but the country was still fantasising about Perkins. On this night in Japan, however, Hackett arose and took his throne.

By now Perkins had retired and joined us in the commentary box as an expert. I was in awe of him. And although everyone on our team knew that I needed to describe the last 25 metres, I wasn't about to start laying down the law of swimming broadcasting to Kieren Perkins.

When it became clear that Hackett wasn't simply going to break the world 1500-metre record but smash it, I made the mistake of asking Kieren a question. He answered it, but then he kept talking. So I only managed to get about five metres of commentary in as Hackett broke Perkins' world record by seven seconds.

For me, it was most disappointing. My job was to capture history, and this was the most historic thing I'd ever seen in the sport. But because of my respect for a champion, I missed the bus.

I must say that Hackett is, in many ways, unlucky. At nearly any other time he could have been the champion from 200 metres through to 1500 metres. His greatest achievement came in 2004 at the Olympic Games in Athens, when he claimed gold with a partially collapsed lung.

Yet there can be no dispute that Thorpe is the best I've ever seen – and probably the best the world has ever seen. That kind of comment normally arouses the emotions, particularly from those who saw Dawn Fraser. I've no doubt the girl from Balmain was great. The great American, Mark Spitz, also stakes a claim, but really Thorpe's achievements are astonishing. He swam the 100 metres, the 200 metres, the 400 metres and the 800 metres. He was the world champion from the 200 metres through to the 800 metres, and the world record holder in each event. He was the Olympic champion at 400 metres as well, and was a vital cog in the Australian men's relay teams. Thorpe is the best Australian swimmer ever. That's my view.

When Thorpe made up his mind to do something, he invariably did it. Take the trials for the Australian championships in Hobart in 2001. Thorpedo decided to include the 100 metres in his program. Until then, Michael Klim had been a lay-down misère as one of the two 100-metre freestylers who would win selection. It's history now that Thorpe won the 100-metres trial, Ashley Callus came home with silver and Klim was denied the chance of swimming the event at Fukuoka. It's that hunger, that determination, that made Thorpe such a danger.

There was some anxiety among the executives that following the Sydney Olympics the popularity of the sport might start to drop off, and that the 2001 World Championships in Fukuoka would be a ratings disaster. How wrong can you be? Those worlds again dominated the ratings battle, as Thorpe won six gold medals and broke three individual world records. Hackett smashed Perkins' 1500-metre world record by an amazing seven seconds.

By this time swimming had become – both to me and to the network – almost as important as rugby league. Nine could now boast that it held the rights to the big four: NRL, AFL, cricket and swimming. Who would've thought that swimming would ever rate alongside events like Grand Finals, State of Origins and Melbourne Cups?

Ratings are one thing, but one of the most satisfying moments of calling it came a few nights after Thorpe beat Hackett at the Australian champs in Hobart in 2001. I was sitting in a tent, having a meal, and executive producer Lesley Tapsall came in and said Ian Thorpe's father, Ken, wanted to speak with me.

'Really?' I asked. 'What for?'

Ken Thorpe was just an ordinary, salt-of-the-earth bloke. 'I just wanted to thank you for the nice things you've been saying about my boy,' he said.

Just as I would years later, when Hazem El Masri said the same sort of thing to me, I teared up again!

19

THE BIG C

I woke up one night in the week leading up to the 2010 Grand Final between the Roosters and the Dragons, and I knew straight away that something wasn't right. I was sweating profusely one minute, then freezing cold the next. I was shaking. I tried to go to the toilet and it was absolute agony trying to urinate.

I went back to bed, but the next morning I was on the doctor's doorstep. He figured out very quickly that I had a urinary tract infection, which he thought might be related to some prostate trouble. My temperature was over 40 degrees, which was dangerous. He told me to take some strong antibiotics. I agreed, but I also told him I had a Grand Final to call.

'Double the dose,' he said. 'We need to get this into

you quick. Come back to me tomorrow morning, and if you haven't shown any improvement then I'll have to put you in hospital on an intravenous drip. That's the only way we'll get you to the Grand Final.'

So I went into Westmead Hospital the next day and saw a specialist. I was still running a dangerously high temperature. Tests soon confirmed the infection. My PSA test – a guide to estimate the risk that cancer is present or is likely to develop in the future – was up alarmingly, from two to 44. The urinary tract infection had indeed been triggered by something going wrong with my prostate.

So I lay there as they fed antibiotics into me intravenously for the next few days. Come Friday, two days before the Grand Final, I called for the doctor. 'I've got to get out of here,' I told him. 'I've got a Grand Final to call.'

'You're not going anywhere,' he said. 'Not until we get your temperature down to where we want it to be. I'll come and see you tomorrow, and if it's down we'll see about letting you go.'

I had called every Grand Final for Nine since 1992, but there was a distinct possibility I was going to miss this one. Luckily, the PSA test came down, and so did my temperature, so they let me out on Grand Final eve.

The problem, though, was that I had no control of my bladder. I could now urinate but I had no control over when.

'What am I going to do about this?' I asked the doc. 'I've got to call the football.'

'The nurses will fit you out with some napkins,' he said.

Napkins? As in nappies. They made me look like I was getting ready for a sumo wrestling match. The next day, I was getting dressed to go to the Grand Final. I put the 'napkin' on, then tried to pull on my jeans. They wouldn't fit and I couldn't do up the belt. Besides that, I looked ridiculous – like a Teletubby. I had to wear tracksuit pants because nothing else would fit.

So off I went to the 2010 NRL Grand Final, between the Dragons and the Roosters, wearing a nappy. As I called that match, with the Dragons mounting a second-half comeback to win an emotional premiership, I was urinating the whole time, and I had no control over it. I knew I was going, I just didn't have a say in the matter. Funnily enough, this was something I had actually experienced before, as I've told you: that Amco Cup game I called with Frank Hyde, when I missed the bottle and pissed down the side of my bloody trousers.

Telling Sterling or Gould what was going on would've been the silliest thing I could have done. So I told nobody until after the event.

In those types of situations, you lean on your professionalism. One time I was calling a trots race at Harold Park and there was a bomb threat. 'Everybody out!' But I kept calling the race. The same thing happened at the Horden Pavilion when I was calling the Australian Indoor Tennis Championships for Channel Ten alongside John Newcombe. There was a fire alarm but we kept going. (That wasn't bravery, by the way – it was instinct mixed with stupidity!)

So I got through the Grand Final but I still had a problem. For the next eight months, I was regularly off to see the doctor with fresh blood tests. The PSA was slowly coming down. After about eight months, and my fourth visit, he said it was down to 5.3.

'That's good for my age, isn't it?' I said.

'I'd still like to do a biopsy,' he said.

So that's what we did.

On 6 June 2011, I was on the back patio, standing at the barbeque, cooking some chops and sausages. It was about 6.30 pm. My mobile rang – it was the doctor. 'You've got some prostate cancer,' he said.

I went numb. I forgot the chops. I forgot the sausages. Swallowed hard a few times. Tears were dripping down my cheeks. I walked inside and saw Cher. 'I've got prostate cancer.'

She had the ability to bring me into line. She's always been more optimistic than me. 'Okay, we've hit a hurdle,' she said. 'We'll get over it and get on to the next one. We'll see the doctor tomorrow.'

We did exactly that. 'What would you do?' I asked him.

'I'd have it out,' he said. 'I've got a position vacant next Monday.'

'What are the ramifications of that?'

'Probably incontinence and impotence.'

'I'm just a kid from Junee, doc,' I said. 'Can you translate?'

'You might lose control of your bladder, and you might never get an erection again.'

I looked at Cher. I might never get an erection again? I wasn't ready to rack the cue just yet.

'Well, that doesn't worry me,' she said, unprompted.

'Thanks very much,' I said.

I was devastated, and now I had this blow to my ego. I mean, what a rap. But it was clear what I had to do.

'Book me in,' I told the doctor.

I knew that news of this would leak out eventually, so I went to management at Channel Nine and Triple M and spoke to them. I wanted to control the story.

When it got wide publicity over the next two or three days, some very wise people contacted me, from out of nowhere, and it was a godsend. They were Alan Jones; Alan Joyce, the boss of Qantas; Wayne Swan, the deputy prime minister; and – from left-field – Michael Stone, the former rugby league referee.

They all had one thing in common, and one message for me: go and see Professor Phil Stricker at St Vincent's Hospital. 'He's the best,' they said.

The NSWRL chief executive Geoff Carr also became involved. He knew Stricker's clinical nurse, Jayne, and he also advised me to contact him. Alan Jones is one of my heroes. But I didn't know Joyce and I didn't know Swan. It was a big surprise to hear from these men, but I was very grateful.

I went to see Professor Phil Stricker, and Cher and my daughter Holly were with me when we walked in to his rooms. I will never forget what his receptionist said. 'Now you're here, you're going to be okay,' she told me.

I will never forget those words. Being a hypochondriac, my first reaction through all of this was: 'When am I going to die? How many days have I got left?' I was thinking the most pessimistic things you can think of. But the receptionist's words made me feel relieved. For a nanosecond, at least.

Then I met Stricker himself. In his consulting rooms, he looked at the results of my biopsy and my bone scan. He was very confident. 'This isn't really urgent,' he said. 'You haven't got that much of it. This biopsy has returned a low reading. They've taken 18 cores, and they've only found cancer in one core. There's no urgency in this. I'm off to the Mediterranean. My mate's got a boat and I'm going to sail with him for six weeks. See you when I get back.'

'Mate, I'm thinking I'm dying,' I said. 'And you're going up to the Mediterranean for a holiday?'

'Mate, it's not bloody urgent,' he said.

I liked it when he swore. I thought, *I've got a brother in arms here. He's on the same wavelength as me.* The first thing I did was cancel the operation. But three weeks into Stricker's holiday, I started to get a bit nervous. I phoned his clinical nurse, Jayne.

'It's Ray Warren,' I said. 'My nerves are killing me. Phil's on the high seas and I'm here shitting myself.'

'I'll contact him,' she said, but I asked her not to disturb him.

The next day, I was playing a round at Castle Hill Golf Club when my phone rang. I wasn't supposed to have my phone on the course; I'd already received a fortnight's suspension for using it a couple of months earlier. But I took this phone call anyway.

'It's Phil Stricker,' the doc said. 'I'm calling from the French Riviera. I hear you're getting nervous.'

'I'm very nervous.'

'I told you not to worry. It's not urgent.'

'That's easy for you to say. I've had a recommendation to see a doctor called David Malouf. Do you mind if I do that?'

'I know him well,' Stricker said. 'He's a good bloke. But I'll still expect to see you when I get back.'

By now, my news had spread through my circle of friends, and Ron Massey had called me to tell me about David Malouf – who, it turned out, had been the ball boy at Cronulla when his father, Peter, was the long-time club doctor. So I went and saw the former Sharks ball boy and president of the Urological Society of Australia and New Zealand.

'There's not a lot here,' Malouf explained. 'You've got a Gleason score of seven. That's a number we don't know what to do with. Four parts are good, but three parts are bad. I think you can fit into a group we call the "active surveillance" group. We don't do anything with you, we just keep you monitored with regular blood tests and biopsies.'

Malouf and Stricker both wanted me to have an MRI. It showed my prostate was enlarged, but it didn't look too bad. Stricker then asked if he could send a part of the cancerous tissue to a firm in America to get its diagnosis on the cancerous part that had been found. So off went this tissue to America. The report came back quite good, he told me, and there was a good chance I wouldn't have too much trouble with it at all. It might never again raise its head – pardon the pun.

So that's where I am today: under surveillance. Do I feel comfortable? When you know you've got some cancer, you're never comfortable. But I don't walk around thinking about it constantly. What does remind me of it are the number of blokes who come to me and seek advice on what to do, and who want to tell me their stories. And I have to be big enough and strong enough to listen to those stories. I have to lend a sympathetic set of ears, or give them the advice that I received: go and get a second opinion, or even a third opinion, before you do anything.

I remember a mate called me while I was still thinking about having my prostate removed.

'Have they done you yet?' he asked. 'Don't let them touch you. I'm 75 and it's ruined my life.'

Prostate cancer is treatable, manageable and curable – that's the slogan they use. Most aged men will take prostate cancer to the grave; that's another one. They'll have died with it, not from it. Statistics say that seven out of ten men in their 70s have it. I'm one of the lucky ones, because the doctors know I've got it. I'm not on any medication, and my PSA levels have been consistent in the three or so years since I was diagnosed.

There are several forms of treatment. There's radiotherapy. There's brachytherapy, which is the insertion of a seed that radiates and attacks whatever cancer is there. Michael Hagan, the former Knights and Parramatta coach, has had that. And then there's removal. That's what Darryl Brohman had. Because he was a young man, and he had a significant amount of it, removal was the best option.

Even if the cancer never flares up again, it's always in the back of my mind. So it comes down to whether I can handle it or not. The first doctor, who had told me to take it out, had been treating me for eight months. He'd got to know me well, and he didn't think I had the character to handle the thought that I had some cancer in me. In other words, he didn't think I could handle being in the surveillance category.

A lot of people I don't know approach me to talk about prostate cancer. It's like breast cancer for men, I've heard it said, and there is a lot of it out there.

When I flew to London for the 2012 Olympic Games, I was in first class and I noticed Alan Joyce sitting in seat 1A.

'My name's Ray Warren,' I said, extending my hand. 'I want you to know how much I appreciated your phone call last year when I really needed people to lean on. I needed help and you were there for me.'

I want to be the same person for others. I was talking to Wally Lewis about this same thing. He's in a similar position because he suffered from epilepsy. He told me how he enjoys talking to people who have it, and talking them through it. I feel the same way.

The ones who upset me the most are those who either don't want to listen or who then start telling me why I'm wrong. All that tends to do is destabilise me mentally. I want to help as many as I can. But I don't need them placing doubts in my head that my decisions are wrong. After all, it is my faith in my doctors that keeps me normal.

I don't get embarrassed talking about it to other men. I don't get embarrassed talking about it to anybody. Because

I see now that I've got the chance to comfort other people. A lot of people, like me on that fateful night in June 2011, think it's a death sentence.

It's not.

20

CAST IN BRONZE

I t started as a joke, and then became one of the most significant things ever to happen to me. I can't tell you how proud I am of it – it's not funny. And how deeply indebted I am to those who made it happen.

That honour belongs to the *Continuous Call Team* on 2GB, the long-standing weekend rugby league show featuring Ray 'Bolts' Hadley, Bob 'Bozo' Fulton, Steve 'Blocker' Roach and Darryl 'Big Marn' Brohman. 'What about giving Rabs a statue in Junee?' one of them once jokingly suggested.

From there, it just snowballed. They started badgering Lola Cummins, the mayor of Junee, and her council, asking why a statue of Rabs was yet to be built. Little did they realise that Laurie Daley, the former Australia, New South Wales and Canberra star, was a much bigger local name than me. And what about Bernie Fraser, the former boss of the Reserve Bank? What about Dr John Potts, the local doctor who had looked after the entire town for the best part of his life?

Anyway, I went along with the joke. Hadley and co. would ring me every Saturday afternoon with an update on the statue, and I would play along with it. Then it started to get a bit serious. It started to worry me that this crazy idea was now growing legs.

So I drove to Junee. I went to the cemetery and visited Mum and Dad, then I went to see Lola. 'This can't happen,' I told her. 'It's embarrassing to me because of all the other people who have done far more significant things for Junee.'

'Ray, I thought it was only a joke,' she said.

'So did I. But I can't put the fire out. You're going to have to stop it.'

'That won't be hard. We can't afford it anyway.'

'There's the answer,' I said, relieved. 'I don't want it, because I'm not entitled to it.'

When I got back to Sydney, I phoned Hadley. 'I've got ya,' I told him. 'I've been to Junee, I've spoken to council. It won't go ahead because they can't afford it, and I don't want it to go ahead anyway.'

A day later, he called me. 'Got ya back,' he said. 'Gyngell is going to underwrite it.'

He was talking about David Gyngell, the chief executive of Channel Nine. I won't repeat what I said to Hadley, but I wasn't pleased.

On Saturday 6 August 2011, in Dobbyn Park in the middle of Junee, my mind started to change. It was raining cats and dogs. The weather was miserable. Both 2GB and Triple M were broadcasting from the park where the statue was to be unveiled. *The Continuous Call Team* did their program in the afternoon, after Dan Ginnane, Billy Birmingham and I had broadcast *Dead Set Legends* in the morning.

The unveiling coincided with the Riverina schoolboys' rugby league carnival, which is the biggest carnival for schoolkids in the world. It started in 1943 – the year I was born – and I first played in it when I was eight. To be honest, I was probably standing back and calling the game instead of playing it.

So the town was at capacity. You couldn't get a park anywhere, in places where you could normally fire a cannon and you wouldn't hit anybody. I didn't know whether they were there for the carnival or the unveiling. Dobbyn Park was a mud heap, as thousands of people crammed in.

Some of my old schoolmates were there, including Neil Taprell. I hadn't seen him since I left school in 1957. A lot of Mum's friends were also there. Most of my living family had come, which made the event so special for me.

Sadly, my older brother Bob was not there. He is one of my heroes, and the apple of my eye. I had total respect for him, and whatever he did I tried to emulate. I had little chance of that, though, because he was a very, very strong bugger, who was equally talented at rugby league and at Australian Rules football.

He played in the second row for Newtown in the late 1950s. He and a crop of reserve-graders were elevated to first grade when the Newtown first-grade side went on strike, wanting more money. So he got to play some first grade in the era of the great John Raper, Barry Harris, Frank Farrington and Dick Poole. Johnny and Bob were quite good friends.

Although Bob was in the police force, and in fact earned the Queen's award for bravery, he always wanted to come back to the country. He went to Cooma in the mid-1960s, and captained Eden-Monaro at the country championships in 1964–65.

I would've loved to have had him there, just like I would've loved to have had Mum and Dad there, too. And my sister June. They had all passed on, but they would've been proud, because this honour was about the whole family.

My sister Gwen, who sadly passed away late in 2013, was there and she just loved it. She became the unofficial publicity agent for the whole thing. Seeing the smile on her face, and the smiles on the faces of my other sisters and my brother Jack, the joy they got from it, convinced me it was time to go along with the whole thing. Joke or no joke, it was time to embrace it, because there was so much sincerity and emotion attached to it.

David Gyngell was there. So was the NSW premier, Barry O'Farrell, who did the unveiling. 'This statue sums up the opportunity that's always existed across this state and across this nation,' he told the crowd. 'Here was a bloke who remains a humble man, who grew up in humble circumstances, who early in life had a dream and worked very had to realise that dream. Who had a few stumbles along the way.'

When it was my turn to speak, I struggled to keep my emotions in check. 'Today is undoubtedly one of the most humbling days of my life,' I said. 'I'm nervous, I've got a lump in my throat, and it won't go away. As a kid, I dreamt of one day becoming a sports commentator. That might sound simple enough, but coming from a small country town like Junee, that ambition was like dreaming the impossible dream. Dreams are not reserved for the rich and the famous. They are there for us all to enjoy, and this statue, in many ways, says it all. If you pursue your dreams, with vigour, passion, energy and desire, not always but just sometimes dreams can come true, and they can happen to you.

'Recently, I was diagnosed with prostate cancer, and naturally my emotions dropped as low as they could be. But today they've been lifted to a level I haven't experienced before. So stuff the cancer, now I've got a statue!'

A few months after the unveiling of the statue, some of my family wanted to take photos with me beside it. So we gathered the family together in Junee and visited the park.

We were taking a few photos when two caravans pulled up across the road. Mum and Dad and kids alighted and came over to take photos as well – and they were quickly baffled by the likeness of this bloke taking photos with his family! They were looking at the statue and then at me, and eventually they asked: 'Is that you or are you a lookalike?' I told them the truth, and they asked if they could take some photos of their own with me, which we did.

When we got back to Sydney, our washing machine

refused to work so we called the whitegoods repairman. He showed up, and the first thing he wanted to do was to show us a photo on his phone of this family having their pics taken alongside me in Junee two days earlier! It turned out that the bloke we'd met there was this guy's brother-in-law, and he'd put a caption on the photo: 'How good is this!'

The fridge mechanic then asked: 'Can I have my photo taken with you as well? In front of the washing machine?' He took the snap of me, Cher and him in front of the washer and sent it off with the caption: 'Anything you can do, I can do better!'

Even though the statue started as a joke, when I go to Junee now and see it, I know the joy it brings to members of my family. I see it as a tribute to the Warren family. Mum and Dad would have been absolutely stoked.

And it's also a reminder that no matter where you come from, no matter how humble your upbringing, no matter what disadvantages you've faced, if you've got the passion and the desire to reach for your dream, then it's achievable. That's what it represents.

It's a nice story for a little town like Junee. I hope it reaches kids like I once was, and speaks to them.

Don't worry about living in a town of 3000 people,

and your mum and dad not having a lot of money. Don't worry if you haven't had a good education, and if you live in a small weatherboard house with no hot water. You can adapt. I found marbles and made them horses. And I did it every afternoon. It doesn't matter where you come from. You can make it.

That statue stands there, I hope, as a reminder of that.

★

The moment the statue was unveiled, the most talked about part of it was: *Does it really look like him?*

When you learn about how it's done, you'll realise that creating a statue from bronze is a tricky process. I had to get a plaster cast of my head months in advance. That was real scary. They put plasticine all over my head, leaving just enough room for me to breath through my nostrils, and then then let it set. I would've sat there for an hour.

The last thing I said to one of Ray Hadley's offsiders, Robert Smith – or 'the Duck', as he's known – was this: 'I'll tell you something. I'm about to be rendered helpless. If anyone takes a photo of me in this situation, I'll have you in court and this whole exercise will be cancelled.'

Then I was introduced to the bloke whose job it was to cover my head in wax. 'The same applies to you and your offsider here,' I said. 'If this gets out, this is all over. You clear?'

When the mould set, it was like a piece of rubber. They just peeled it off me like an orange skin. When they were pulling it off, I thought my snozza was going as well. Then they measured my arms, legs, neck . . . it was an amazingly long and intensive process.

So I was a bit surprised when, after the premier unveiled it, a few people asked me if they thought the finished product resembled me. I only engaged in that conversation five or six times. I thought it looked like me, but you need to remember it's cast in bronze. It's hard to get the hair right. Anyway, I didn't really care. All I cared about was what it symbolised.

When I was on my way home from Junee to Sydney the next day, I heard some rumblings from the warfront. Apparently Andrew Voss had asked the panel on *The Sunday Roast* if the statue looked like me. That was all I ever knew about it.

Ray Hadley was also driving home, I later found out, and someone phoned him to tell him that Voss had bagged the statue. Whether they gave him the right or wrong information,

I don't know. But, Bolts being Bolts, he then got on the air and proceeded to give Andrew a bollocking.

Vossy called me later that Sunday. I was in the backyard at home in Sydney, watering some plants at the time. 'I just want you to watch and listen to the program before you make a judgement,' he said.

'Andrew, I'm getting second-hand and third-hand accounts of all this,' I said. 'Mate, I won't be listening to anything or watching anything, because I don't really care what people think.' That was God's truth. I walked away from Junee as the proudest man alive, and I still am. I don't care what people think of it.

Bolts reacted as you would expect, given how much effort he had put into it. Okay, it had started as a joke but he knew better than anyone how much work and how many people had contributed to it. He wasn't amused that someone at Channel Nine would criticise the statue.

From there it snowballed. Vossy took legal action against Ray and 2GB for what he said. The case was settled out of court, and Andrew has since moved on from Channel Nine.

21

BOLTS

I am not sure when he got the nickname or who gave it to him, but 'Bolts' is the moniker by which Ray Hadley is often known. Apparently it relates to *The Munsters* – Herman Munster, I believe.

I feel I must explain this because of the number of times people have confused me with him. If Bolts looks like Herman Munster, then it's hard to fathom the comparison – in looks, anyway. I look like a lot of things, and I've often been told so, but Herman Munster has never been one of them.

I was once asked to speak to a group of retirees at a Probus Club meeting. Basically, they were all people my own age. I'd spoken to the MC on the phone several times. He called me Ray and I called him Fred, but on the day he introduced me like this: 'Today, ladies and gentlemen, we have with us one of Australia's leading broadcasters, Mr Ray Hadley.'

To say I was embarrassed would be an understatement, but the audience members were beside themselves with laughter. The old MC was distraught, so I pacified him with a few stories. 'Mate,' I said, 'don't worry about it.'

On one occasion I was approached at a service station. An older man asked if I would pose for a photograph with his granddaughter.

'Sure,' I said. 'No worries.'

'I really love listening to your morning radio show,' he said.

'Sorry, I think you've got me mixed up with Ray Hadley,' I said. 'I'm Ray Warren. I call the football.'

Before I could blink, he snatched up his little girl, who was standing next to me, and literally fled to his car. I was left standing there like a paedophile.

Another time, I went to see the rectal surgeon about a minor matter that I had in that part of the anatomy.

'Let me examine you,' he said. 'Get up on the couch, put your knees under your chin and face the wall.' Seconds later, he said, 'I can fix this, but I'll need some help from the nurse.'

She came into the room.

'Do you recognise this bloke?' he asked her.

'Well, from this angle, not really,' she said. 'But I heard his voice out in the waiting room and he sounds like Ray Hadley.'

I remember screaming into the wall, with my knees under my chin. 'I'm not Ray Hadley!'

The way Bolts tells it, his first contact with me was in the mid-1980s, when he dropped a cassette tape into my letterbox. Until then, he'd been driving cabs and auctioneering but he desperately wanted a career in radio and sports broadcasting. During Parramatta's run of premierships in the early 1980s under coach Jack Gibson, he would sit on the sidelines and commentate into a tape recorder, just as I had done.

I openly admit that I never listened to his tape, and I never got back to him. He still often brings it up. I jokingly say, 'I lived at number 25 and you put it in number 52!' The real reason was his timing: he'd caught me in the middle of the most dramatic time of my life. This was all around the time I left Channel Ten, which happened just after I'd split up with my wife.

I know I overlooked some things at that time of my life,

and for that I'm sorry. Listening to Ray's tape was one of those things I simply didn't have the headspace to think about.

Of course, as it turned out, he didn't need my help or advice. At Sydney radio stations 2UE and then 2GB, he and Alan Jones have been a lethal left-right punch for Macquarie Radio and its owner, John Singleton.

Singo is a friend who confided in me many years ago. 'You know, Rabs,' he said, 'there's only one thing in life I'd like to do, and that's own a radio station.' He obviously forgot that he would like to marry several times and get divorced as many times, but that's life.

Now, he owns two stations, and they couldn't be any more different. On one station, you've got Alan and Bolts. And on the other, 2CH, you've got the legendary Bob Rogers, who plays golden oldies.

Hadley has strong opinions, and he's also got access to a microphone seven times a week – on radio and on television, on Channel Nine. He's not frightened to express his firm opinions, whether he is right or wrong.

We play golf occasionally in a group with Dickie, Kevin and Milton. They love having me and Hadley play with them – they call us the Ping wood ducks, since Ping sponsor us both. I think that means we are no good! The people at

Ping have never seen us play, and thank God for that. The sponsorship won't last very long if they ever do.

In the wash-up of the Andrew Voss saga, David Gyngell appointed Ray to call some football at Nine. When he asked, I said: 'It's different to radio. That's what you will discover. One audience can see the match, the other cannot. The hardest thing you will find is measuring how many words you use.'

That was foreign to me when I moved from radio to television. I thought you had to fill up the air with a lot of words. There are times when I do use a lot of words, but I'm just doing that to build up the excitement. You'll never hear me using a lot of words when there's nothing happening. A radio broadcaster has to fill up any dead air, but a television broadcaster can let the pictures speak for themselves. That's the difference.

It comes down to this thing I call 'light and shade'. It is what I'm all about as a caller, and it rules how I call a game of football. If you listen to the crowd, they'll tell you when to be 'light' and when to be 'shade'. The crowd is the governor of my excitement levels. When they're standing up and cheering, I need to be doing the same in the broadcast box. That's light. But I'm never out of the chair when a team is rucking it out off their own line. That's shade.

No piece about Ray Hadley is complete without addressing the many feuds he has been involved in over the years. We had a fair one ourselves, once upon a time. Unfortunately, he hasn't always seen eye to eye with a couple of my long-term workmates. Being in the middle of that has been difficult. But it's interesting: nowadays they are back working together, so perhaps the healing process is happening.

Arguments between certain sections of the rugby league media are frequent, and the hatred can run deep. It is not like the old days, when I was just starting out. There was Frank Hyde, Tiger Black and John O'Reilly. They were three absolute gentleman, and we were all great friends.

One day at Lidcombe Oval, my radio leads from the perimeter fencing were not quite long enough to get me to the card table on the sideline. With a pair of pliers, Frank quickly spliced some spare leads he had with him and extended me out to where I could see and call the game. That's the way it was back then. I wish that was still the norm rather than the exception.

I recall how, on a Kangaroo tour, two opposing journos would take the same day off during the week, agreeing that neither would scoop the other while they enjoyed their rest day. Bill Mordey from the *Mirror* and Ernie Christensen from the *Sun* would make this pact, and Bill would head for the casino, and Ernie to the dogs. They were both brilliant journos, as were Ian Heads and Alan Clarkson. I don't recall any animosity, pot-shots or bickering.

22

LONDON CALLING

Most sports broadcasters believe the pinnacle of their career is to cover an Olympic Games. I never felt like that. My dream was to call the races, the football and the tennis.

The only time I ever mildly thought about being involved in an Olympics was the 1984 Games in Los Angeles, when Ten wanted me to anchor its broadcast. I didn't have any regrets about not doing that until I was fired a few years later, when it suddenly seemed like a really bad career move. The fear of getting on that plane to Los Angeles, the fear of thinking the whole world was on my shoulders if this thing failed, the fear of sports that were foreign to me – it was all driving me crazy.

After 1984, it didn't matter. The Seven Network commandeered the Games for the next two decades after Ten had the rights in Seoul in 1988. Aside from the Sydney Games in 2000, it didn't particularly worry me that I wasn't calling the Olympics because I didn't work for Seven. I was working for the network I always wanted to – Nine – and that was all that mattered. That was my path, and I wasn't moving from it.

Then, in October 2007, things changed. I was on *Dead Set Legends* on Triple M one Saturday morning. The producer came into the studio and said that Mike Tancred, the media and communications director for the Australian Olympic Committee, wanted to come on-air to announce that Nine had won the free-to-air broadcast rights for the London Olympics in 2012.

'You better get ready to call the swimming again, Rabs,' Mike said.

'Yeah, good,' I replied. 'You're kidding, aren't you?'

That was the pessimism talking. In 2007, I was 65. I hadn't learnt about the prostate cancer by that stage, but I thought I certainly would have retired from broadcasting by 2012.

The next minute, Eddie McGuire was on the line. Eddie was the chief executive of Channel Nine in those days, and he was the one who secured the rights to the games.

'It's Eddie McGuire, Rabs,' he said. 'I was at Ten when you pulled out of the Games in 1984. We've just won the rights to the Games of 2012. Even if you're in a casket, I'm taking you.'

'Ed, you know I don't really like flying, regardless of whether I'm dead or alive. You know me.'

'You are coming to the Games of 2012. That's it. Dead or alive.'

I didn't think much of it at the time.

In March that year, I had called the World Championships in Melbourne. My offsider for those worlds was a young bloke called Adam Harvey. He was a lovely kid, and he'd been my commentator assistant since 2002. He was unassuming, very diligent, well researched, and he did everything he could possibly do to bring me up to speed with stats and pronunciations. You name it and he did it for me. He was my left-hand and right-hand man.

He phoned as soon as I came off air. 'You're coming, aren't you?' he asked.

I gave him the same sermon. 'Adam, you know me pretty well. I don't like flying. I don't like being away from home. By then, I'll be 68. Life is a very funny thing. You can't predict it. I can't answer your question.'

He peppered me with the same question a few times after that. 'You're definitely coming to London, aren't you?' he'd say.

'Time will tell,' I'd reply. 'Life can be cruel.'

I never mixed socially with Adam much. He was in his 20s when we first met, and I was in my 60s. I just knew how important he was to my success as a swimming commentator. I loved him dearly and I respected him enormously.

I'd never seen him with a partner, but he took a fancy to one of the girls who also worked at Nine. He asked Angela to marry him, and she said yes. When the news broke, I thought it was fabulous. He'd found someone who wanted to be united with him. I was so happy for him.

A month after Adam got home from working at the 2010 Winter Olympics in Vancouver, he noticed a mark on his leg that looked suspicious. He went to have it checked, and it turned out to be a melanoma.

That was in April 2010. In August of that year, it killed him. He was 33. Unbelievably, his father followed him to the grave not long after, with cancer playing an evil role again.

On the day of Adam's funeral, I had to be at a football match in Brisbane. But I recorded a video message to be played at the service: 'Adam begged me to go to London,'

I said, 'and I fobbed him off with answers like, "Mate, time can be a funny thing", and, "Life can be cruel," and "I don't know where I'm gonna be in 2012."'

All those things I'd bloody said to him, they'd come back to haunt me. Then, at the end of that tribute, I said: 'And so, because he's gonna be looking down, at the London Olympics, he's gonna be looking to see that I'm there. And I will be. I promise you, mate, I will be.'

And that's why I went. At 68, I didn't need to go to London, but that was the inspiration I needed to get on a plane. I would have felt no regret about not going. There was no scratch I had to itch. I knew there would've been pressure on me to go, and, in his own lovely way, Adam had already started doing that before his death. And when Adam died, I had no more excuses.

★

So, a few weeks out from the London Olympics, Cher, Holly and I boarded a plane in Sydney. We were on an A380. Nine had spared no expense, putting us in business class. I fly better the further up the front of the plane I am seated. That's not because I'm up myself, I just feel more comfortable. Having accrued many frequent flyer points over the years, I upgraded again to first class.

I'd never flown on an A380 before. I sat there in the first-class lounge looking at it and thought, *Jesus, how's this huge thing gonna get up?* When we took our seats, one of the stewards told me that if I pressed a button, I could watch the plane take off on Sky Cam, which is a video camera mounted on the tail of the plane. I watched us take off, up through the clouds, and for some reason I felt safer. Who'd have thought it?

Those at Nine know I like big planes. I feel comfortable on big planes. The travel company that books our flights, Stage and Screen, knows I'm a rare beast and tries to accommodate my wishes. For me, the plane has got to have a kangaroo on the tail. I won't fly with anyone else but Qantas. I sound like Dustin Hoffman out of that movie *Rain Man*, don't I?

I loved calling the swimming again. I went to the London Aquatic Centre with the belief that I would get the chance to call three gold medals for Australia: Alicia Coutts in the 200-metre individual medley, the men's 4 x 100-metre freestyle relay, and James Magnussen – the man dubbed 'the Missile' – in the 100-metre freestyle, an event in which he was world champion.

My prediction of three gold medals was well below the expectations of most people. But I'd done my research, and that seemed right. I'd gone through the World Championship times from Shanghai, and the trials from Adelaide, and in my opinion three gold would be spot on.

I was calling with Grant Hackett and Giaan Rooney in London. That was a new experience for me, because I'd worked with Duncan Armstrong and Nicole Livingstone my whole career. During one swim during the meet, I mistakenly called Grant 'Duncan'. That's how ingrained Duncan was in my mind!

I had awful audio problems over in London. I was sitting shoulder to shoulder with commentators from all over the world. Because I am computer illiterate, I was constantly referring to my handwritten research, while everyone else was using a computer.

And for that reason, I thought about Adam all the time. I had some wonderful help. But nobody could read what I needed, when I needed it, like him. He'd have a split time in front of me, or a world-record time. Or he'd tell me if a swim was the third-fastest ever in a certain event. He'd even find out the name of a swimmer's pet dog if I wanted it.

History records the Australian team's performance in London as a failure. They look at how Magnussen tanked in the anchor leg of 4 x 100-metre freestyle, and how Australia failed to claim a medal, finishing in fourth, despite all the pre-race trash talk with the Americans, who were spearheaded by Ryan Lochte and possibly the best ever in Michael Phelps. They look at how another American, Nathan Adrian, beat Magnussen by one-hundredth of a second in the 100-metre freestyle. This, despite all the hype and publicity that Magnussen was a near certainty to win the event – much of which came from his own confident mouth.

To be honest, I thought Magnussen was home in the 100 metres. I've always gone with my gut reaction. But he didn't win, by the barest of margins.

One of the most regrettable things about the London Olympics was the nation's failure to properly recognise the gold medal we *did* win: the six girls who enabled Australia to win gold in the women's 4 x 100-metre relay on the first night of the swimming program. Their achievement was monumental, but it was washed away with all this bleeding-heart stuff for the men. At the end of the day, when we should've been showering the women with congratulations, we were worrying about the failure of the men.

Each of those four girls in the final had a story to tell. Cate Campbell had been ruled out for all of 2010 with glandular fever, her career almost crippled by fatigue. Coutts had undergone two operations on her bowel in the four years leading into London. Mel Schlanger had retired, and only 18 months prior to the Olympics hadn't trained because of a viral infection, before mounting a comeback.

Then there was 18-year-old Brittany Elmslie, who had struggled with weight issues and said she'd hit rock bottom a year before the Games. Her third leg put the Australians almost half a second ahead of the United States, allowing them to beat the Dutch to the wall.

It was a great story: they were the only gold medal in the pool. But instead of recognising them, all we did was carry on about how it was a tragedy that Magnussen didn't win.

Let's get something straight: Magnussen lost by a fingernail. If he'd have swum his best time, he'd have won, but the kid from America was too good on the day. What people don't understand is that swimming is a funny sport. You've only got to miss the kick by a tenth of a second or put in a bad turn, and there goes your race. I've called a few races in which there's been one-hundredth of a second between first and second – Giaan Rooney was one of them, but she won.

Australia left London with ten swimming medals – one gold, six silver and three bronze – and the inquisition into what happened went on for months. At one stage, there were three separate inquiries going on, and the term 'toxic culture' kept coming up. It was discovered that members of the 4 x 100-metres freestyle team had used Stilnox at a pre-Games camp in Manchester. People said the athletes' use of social media was to blame for their poor performances.

To me, blaming the Stilnox thing was a cop-out. So was blaming social media. These athletes are the kids of today. Social media might get a homesick kid through the night when he or she is on the other side of the world.

And I don't buy the argument about Magnussen. The events in Manchester impacted on his relay swim, but they didn't impact on his individual swim? Leave me alone. One one-hundredth of a second in the individual? Our problem is we set such high standards for our athletes in various sporting pursuits: sometimes when they don't live up to those standards, we become super-critical.

Take a look at other sports. If you think about some of the great rugby league sides we've seen, the great players came together as a crop. We had that great Maroons backline of Allan Langer and Wally Lewis and Gene Miles and Mal Meninga and Michael Hancock and Willie Carne. Players like them don't come along every year. And look at Parramatta:

Peter Sterling, Mick Cronin, Steve Ella, Eric Grothe, Brett Kenny. The Eels are still trying to achieve what they managed to do in the early 1980s. They set a benchmark, and still nobody can beat it.

In the swimming, during the 1990s and early 2000s Australia had one of its most golden eras, and that is saying something, given how many golden eras and fabulous swimmers we've had. There were Kieren Perkins, Grant Hackett, Ian Thorpe and Susie O'Neill. Then Susie was followed by Petria Thomas. Then you had Michael Klim and Geoff Huegill and Leisel Jones. Now, that's a harvest. They're not going to come up every year. But that doesn't mean that today's coaches or administrators aren't as good, or that the young swimmers who competed in London tried any less.

Swimming has been very good to me. It played a fundamental role in resurrecting my career. Calling it has been one of the highlights of my life, but it also brought one of the saddest moments I've had. The absence of Adam Harvey in London was the biggest vacuum I've experienced in my professional career. I only hope his family get to read this book, to know how much he meant to me. It brings a lump to my throat, even now, as I write in fond remembrance of him.

23

FAMILY MATTERS

The time was the late 1990s. I was walking down the street, not far from our home in Castle Hill, pushing along a stroller. I went past two old girls who were having a chinwag outside their homes. 'Morning, ladies,' I said.

'Grandad's turn to babysit, is it?' they chirped.

'Yeah, good one. Have a nice day.'

I suppose that's what happens when you have a daughter brought into the world when you are 54 years old.

I'm always quite amazed when I hear about young blokes and their babies. I've known of players who have pulled out of Kangaroo tours because they wanted to be there for the birth of their babies. That sort of thing amazes me, because in my day it never happened.

I was there with great anxiety for the birth of Holly, but Cher kicked me out of the delivery room before it happened. Not because I might've called proceedings but because she knew I was hypochondriac, and I wouldn't be able to handle what was about to occur. I was fine with that.

Holly – my youngest child, and only daughter – was born on 11 September 1997. It was a long struggle to conceive her, but it was all worth it. For quite some time she was intrigued by people saying, 'So you're a 9/11 baby? Wow!' She and Cher came with me on a trip to Montreal for the World Swimming Championships in 2005, and we went via New York. We took Holly to visit Ground Zero. I tried to explain, as best I could, just what 9/11 was all about.

I've been lucky enough to be able to be at home a lot with Holly, and to spend a lot of good quality time with her. This time around, I was much older, and I wasn't consumed by my job like I was when I had my two sons in the 1970s.

Now she's a teenager, and her ambition is to be an actress. I don't know what credentials you need but I reckon she'll be brilliant. I'm dreaming of seeing her turn 21.

Holly thinks Cher and I are over-protective, and we probably are because we're much older than most parents.

There aren't many teenagers who would have a 71-year-old father. And if we are over-protective, well, I can't apologise for that. I reckon kids today need more protection than ever, given the temptations out there and the dangers of life as we know it today.

Some people might think having a child when you are up in years is wrong. That's their opinion, but I have found that it's given me a fresh injection of life. It's very invigorating, even though I worry like hell each and every day about whether she will be safe and come home in one piece. I'm very concerned about blokes who appear on the doorstep, particularly those with cars. They are given a fairly good sermon, I can assure you.

I've seen things change so much since I was a kid in the 1940s and 50s. My sons, Chris and Mark, grew up in the 1970s and 80s, and now Cher and I are bringing up Holly during the early part of the next millennium.

The whole experience has given me a chance to understand fatherhood quite differently. I was 21 when I was first married, then 23 when I got into what I wanted to do. Suddenly, I was off, trying to make every post a winner in my career. I lost sight of the important things. I would never say my two boys had a diminished upbringing, but had I not been in the media – if I'd stayed a policeman, for instance – I'd have been there for them a lot more than I was. These days, with Holly, I've been around. I've got more spare time than most fathers.

Mark, my eldest son, is now in his mid-40s. He runs a successful advertising agency called Warren Media. Just as I did, he yearns to be a full-time sports caller. He has had a taste of it over the years, calling the boxing at the Commonwealth Games in British Columbia and the schoolboys' rugby league on television.

He loves the fight game. You'll often see him as the ring announcer at bouts here and overseas. He's a really good caller in his own right, but getting to do precisely what you want to do in life is easier said than done. Although I had my ups and downs, I was one of the lucky ones.

Mark wants to follow in my footsteps, and there's nothing wrong with that. In fact, it is common for kids to want to do what their parents do. But this field of work is extremely limited in its numbers, which makes it incredibly difficult to get into. All of us have frustrations in life. Handling them is the key.

One thing I know about Mark is that he doesn't lack the three ingredients that I see as vital in any endeavour: passion, energy and dedication. In fact, he exhibited all these qualities while convincing me to write this book.

My second son, Chris, is also now in his 40s. Unlike me, he did well both at school and at university, where he completed a diploma in business and marketing. He also did really well at footy, twice playing for NSW Catholic Colleges at the Australian championships, and he won an S.G. Ball Cup for Parramatta in the late 1980s. As I wrote earlier, he went on to be graded with Western Suburbs, and played first grade a few times.

When he was a junior, Chris didn't stand out like some but he was determined to do well. As the better players were attracted to the temptations that kids often are, he would be grinding away at his fitness, diet and skills. That's why he made it and achieved his goals in the game.

Chris had no real desire to be in the media, but as fate had it, he fell into a TV job in England while on holiday. He didn't come back for ten years, and gained much experience. He came home a few years ago to work for Fox Sports as a newsreader. Recently, they made several staff redundant, and unfortunately Chris was one of those who went. But knowing him, he'll bounce back. He and his wife, Sally, now love living in Newport, on the northern peninsula, and they have four kids, Fred, Matilda, Joe and Bobby Ray.

Both Mark and Chris were born just after that part of my life when I had been plodding along as a policeman but really wanted to be a sports commentator. As a dad, I did my best but, as I've said, I was chasing my dream. I'm sure I got many of my priorities wrong in that time. Their mother, Monica, through all of that, was a pillar of strength. She was tireless in looking after the boys. She was great.

Each of my kids has their own personality. Each has had their highs and lows – don't we all? I love them all – that goes without saying. And I hope life brings them the joy it has brought to me.

At the end of the day, a parent's love is not governed by whether your son or daughter becomes a neurosurgeon, a labourer or a shop assistant. None of that matters to those who love you.

I think of the jobs I did before I arrived where I am now . . . I started as an apprentice fitter and turner on the railway. Then I dabbled in the clerical side of the business. In Quirindi I sold tickets. Then I turned to selling insurance, and driving taxis. At one stage I was mowing lawns for my mates. I worked in pubs, behind the bar and picking up glasses.

So when I talk about the frustrations you face when you're striving to do what you want to do, I think I'm qualified to have an opinion. What deepens those frustrations is when you see other people getting jobs through nepotism or through the 'old mates' system. When that happens, it can make the blood boil.

24

THE LAST CALL

At the end of the 2013 season, Andrew Johns gave me a call as he was driving up the F3 Freeway, from Sydney to Newcastle. 'I'm heading up to Newcastle to have a drink to mark Bedsy's retirement,' he explained, referring to Danny Buderus, the Knights hooker whose career had come to an abrupt end early in the match against the Roosters. 'Is there anything you'd like me to say to him on your behalf?'

'Yeah,' I said.

'Why don't you text me what you want to say, and I'll pass it on.'

'But I haven't got your number,' I said.

'It's the one that just came up on your phone,' he pointed

out. 'Send it to that one.'

I hung up from Johnsy, then my eldest niece, Judy, phoned. She's the daughter of my eldest sister, Gwen. 'Mum's had a stroke,' she explained. 'She's no good at all.'

I went out into the back yard to water my tomatoes. That was my way of handling the shock of this news, I suppose. Then I remembered that I hadn't sent Andrew that message. I typed out what I wanted him to say to Danny Buderus on my behalf.

'I want you to know you're one of the nicest people I've met in my life,' I wrote. 'You've been a monumental success in everything you've tried. And everything you've tried, you've achieved. You are still, in my mind, the best hooker I've ever seen.' Then I pressed send.

Later than night, my phone rang and Cher answered it. It was the niece again. 'Is Ray okay?' she asked. 'He sent me a text message saying I'm the best hooker he's ever seen.'

I'd sent the text to her, not to Andrew Johns!

I can handle making mistakes like that; I'm mindless with phones and computers. But making mistakes and not knowing I'm making them is my biggest fear. That's what will make me retire. And if I do retire, what am I going to do then? I haven't read a book in my life.

My longevity at Nine is due to the people I work with. When Gary Burns left the network, I started working with a man who was a young racing journalist when I was a young racecaller. His name is Steve Crawley and he's now the head of sport at Nine. He's a delight to work with. He's passionate beyond belief, and he treats everybody with fairness and respect. He's not one of those blokes who taps you on the shoulder when you've done something wrong, but he's forever patting you on the back when you've done something right.

Another essential part of the coverage is Matt Callander, Kenny's son. For me, having him there makes me think I've died and come back again. He looks like Deafie, he's as deaf as Deafie, but he's got the most placid nature about him, while Deafie talks loudly and raucously. Matthew is just a delight to work with. His ability to handle people, particularly television people, is amazing.

I've also been kept young by doing *Dead Set Legends* on Triple M in Sydney every Saturday morning. The show's now been going for 18 years, making it the longest-running show on FM radio in Australia. I was there on day one.

When I started on the show I was with the former Australian cricketers Michael Whitney and Greg Matthews. Over the years, others on the panel have included H.G. Nelson,

Mark Geyer, Billy Birmingham and Richard Freedman. Gus lasted about five minutes. The show was presented first by Russell Barwick and now by Dan Ginnane.

I love working with Freedman. We spend a lot of our down time talking about racing. I've got him pinned as the kid from the private school, the toff from Melbourne. But in fact his background is in Yass, and a rich grazing family. Everything they touched turned to money. He wears a scarf to work and a tweed jacket with leather patches. (Most of that is my imagination, by the way – I really like him!)

Freedman is always saying how he likes expensive shoes. One day he walked in wearing moccasins with tassels on them. I've got a pair too, and when I wear mine, I get told, 'You know they went out of fashion with Sammy Davis Jr?' But they're my favourite pair of shoes. Mine cost $49 at Payless and I got another pair free. He bought his in England.

Anyway, on this day I found a pair of scissors and hid under the studio console, in among the wiring, while Freedman was in the brasco. He came back in and sat down while Ginnane was reading a commercial. Then I snipped off one of the tassels on his fancy shoes. When he noticed, he exploded: 'These are Bally shoes – they cost me $700! I bought them in Carnaby Street!'

An hour later, I pulled exactly the same trick again. He's a slow learner, obviously!

★

At the start of 2013 David Gyngell called me into his office at Channel Nine. 'Here's a five-year contract,' he said.

'I don't think there's any way in the world I can get to the end of five years, mate,' I told him.

'I don't care if you don't,' he replied. 'But that's my way of saying to you, as I've always said, that the only way you and Richie Benaud go out of here is in a box.'

'That's nice,' I laughed. 'Seriously, mate, it's not the easiest of jobs.'

'Well, Richie's 84.'

'David, you keep comparing me to Richie. On the cricket, you've got nine commentators, and they've got three on, then three off, and they revolve. Richie goes on there for 20 minutes in every hour, and might say, "Marvellous shot, that." Yes, he's a tremendous commentator and everyone hangs on to every word he says, but, David, you should come and stand behind me one night and see what I do for an hour and a half. There is always some chance that my head will explode. The top will come right off my head. It will be like Mount Etna.'

'Righto, I understand. Just sign it, will you?'

As things stand today, I am adamant I won't see out my five-year deal. Just after Christmas in 2013, Cher, Holly and I flew to the Gold Coast for a holiday. We came out of Brisbane into an awfully big cloud, and I sat there gripping the armrest, my knuckles white. I was reminded of this bloody thing that's been a bugbear for my whole life.

I still have this phobia about flying despite the number of trips I've done since joining Nine. I'd have over half a million frequent flyer points, even though I use them all the time. I'm okay on a smooth flight, when I can marvel at the countryside and the fields below: the canola blooming in yellow, the wheat and the oats in green, and the fallow or ploughed brown earth puncturing all of them. I love being at 37,000 feet on a clear day. But when there's turbulence, I am in hell. And I know I have to take flights nearly every second week during the footy season.

So when will I finish calling for good? Holly finishes high school at the end of 2015, and that seems like an appropriate time for me to go. But I'll certainly be happy to go earlier if suddenly I don't think I'm doing the job as well as I can do it. And particularly if someone I trust taps me on the shoulder.

I have to be careful about who I listen to, since there's a whole raft of reasons why someone might say something. It would need to be someone I really trust, who is more concerned about me than himself. I worked with a couple of blokes who were great commentators but who began making mistakes in the latter stages of their careers, and that's what they were remembered for. My greatest fear is finishing like that.

Some people might think this job is easy and glamorous, and that you can do it till you are 100. But let me tell you, although I love it to death, it is a draining job, and not just when I'm at work. People are forever wanting to talk business with me, and that's good – at least they are talking to me – but it means I never really get the chance to leave my work in the broadcasting box.

Talking of stress, my doctor loves his footy and asked whether he could come and watch me broadcast a match from the commentary booth. He was amazed at the excitement levels I reached and what my blood pressure must have been. At the end of the night, he said, 'Now I know what I've been treating all these years.'

People often come up to me and say things like, 'Please don't go – don't retire. The game won't be the same without you.' That is so humbling and flattering, but because of my inherent paranoia those generous comments also remind me that the day I leave is not so far away.

The whole thought of retirement frightens me. I struggle to think what I will do to fill in the time. But I don't want to go out bumbling and fumbling like an old fart, undoing the good work that I hope I have done.

I guess I would like to leave the job having called the best try I have ever seen. Like Mark Coyne on the end of those 11 sets of hands, or Billy Slater from a kick, kick and catch. Or Brett Mullins or Eric Grothe or Greg Inglis . . . If I still have the ability to recognise the greatness of a moment like those, that would be magic.

As I said earlier in this book, no one is indispensable. Who takes over from me when I go? I don't know, and in some ways I don't care. Well, I do but I will have no say in the matter. As long as they bring to the job the same respect and love that I have, I will be happy.

When I put the microphone down at the end of the 1986 Grand Final and then broke down and cried, I didn't believe I was at a crossroads – I thought I was at the end. Twenty years after the moment I had that first bet on Playboy, listening to Ken Howard on the radio, I was standing next to him in a broadcast box. And then for the next 20 years after that, I lived the dream, then it came to an end.

But it didn't really. When I look back now, I know that this was the launching pad I needed. Although it put me into six years of isolation and divorced me from my dream, it also made me realise that I would do anything to get back to that place. I came out of the experience as a better human being. I was aware of how fragile life in the media could be – and how brutal.

Now, I'm hugely satisfied, and I'm proud of what I've achieved. I've learnt to treat people better. And as a commentator, I became better. I'm an honouree of the Men of League, I'm a Paul Harris fellowship member of Rotary, their highest award, I've won Logies . . . I've got a statue, for heaven's sake! I've got all those things to look back on, and it all came during my second chance.

Just days before this book went to print, a letter arrived from Government House. *What have I done now?* I thought.

'The Governor-General wishes to inform you that you have been awarded the Medal of the Order of Australia. You are now entitled to use the initials OAM after your name.'

I was blown away by this. I never set out for any recognition, from anyone, for anything I've done.

I never thought that this ambition of mine, this dream, would take me to where I am today. Sometimes I pinch myself and think, *Jesus, I've got kids pulling me up in the street, asking for photos and high-fives, doing impersonations of me* – it's bloody amazing!

I signed off from my broadcast of the 1986 Grand Final on a solemn note. 'I'm low on regret,' I said, 'and high on disappointment.'

Now, as I write these final words, I can tell you that I've forgotten about the regrets, and I can live with the disappointments. This has been a beautiful journey!

AFTERWORD

BY PHIL GOULD

I f you've survived the book and come this far, perhaps
you will be prepared to come a little further.

Everything you have read so far in this book is
absolutely true. Well, at least according to Ray it's all true.
I sense he has told these stories so often over the years that
even the obvious embellishments in these yarns have become
reality in his mind.

I have heard all these stories a thousand times over. The
marbles down the wooden slope, the police force, his football
days, his first bet on Playboy, his days as a racing commentator, the great Ken Howard, Bert Bryant, his golf . . .

Every time we drive through Melbourne, Rabs takes
us past the old public swimming baths where he earned his
bronze medallion. The Tony Roche tennis yarn cracks me

up. The stories I love most are those about his gambling exploits. The first time I met Ray was on a racecourse. To be honest, I hope I live to hear them all a thousand times more.

Whether we're travelling together in a car or on a plane, waiting around at the football, enjoying a few beers together after work or having dinner in a nice restaurant with our families, Ray's storytelling is always outstanding entertainment and the highlight of any time we spend together.

Once you get him wound up with a few chardonnays under his belt, he can relate story after story from his past – each one with a classic punchline or a hilarious look at his colourful life. Some of it is hard to believe. If I hadn't been there on any number of occasions, I wouldn't have believed the stories either.

The story about him losing the trifecta on protest at Rosehill that day is one of my favourites. I was there. He told this young guy who was working the bar area and picking up empty glasses that he would pay him double his wages if he quit his job for the afternoon and just looked after Ray and his friends with drinks. He pulled the kid's bow tie off and declared, 'You're working for me now, son.'

You should've seen the look on his face when the protest was upheld and he lost the money he thought he'd won.

Actually, it wasn't the money he lost that concerned him most. He was more worried about having to pay the guy's wages, as he had promised. I really shouldn't laugh. It's a terrible feeling when you lose a race on protest. But this time it was priceless!

I love the yarns where he is calling a race where he has also had a bet, and the only horse he knows in the race is the one he's backed. Or the time he was commentating at a provincial meeting and missed the start of a race because he was down in the betting ring, trying to get the top odds about his selection. He raced up to the commentary box as the horses turned into the home straight and grabbed the microphone. He pretended it hadn't been working! 'Testing . . . Testing . . . Testing,' he started. 'Oh, good, we're back on air.' He then called the final 200 metres of the race as though nothing had happened.

It's easy to find fault with Ray – mainly because he tells you about his faults every time you see him. He is brutally honest about himself. He is fiercely loyal and protective of family and friends, but he's not so kind to himself. He tells you about himself, warts and all.

For the record, I love Ray Warren. He is a mentor, a confidant, a mate. I enjoy every minute of the time I work with him. I cherish the time we and our families get to spend together socially, when we're away from the ears of the public.

Like him, the question I am most often asked is: 'Do you and Rabbits actually hate each other, or is all that stuff put on?'

'All that stuff', of course, refers to the sometimes heated and argumentative banter we generate during our football commentary for Channel Nine. I guess most of that is my fault. I drive him crazy. More about this a little later.

★

I have known Ray for many, many years. My introduction to him came back in the 1960s, when he was calling greyhound races at Wentworth Park and Harold Park in Sydney. He was the man with the deep, raspy voice and the fluent, stylish expression.

I first met Ray at the racetrack. Then at every racetrack. Every week.

In the 1970s and '80s Ray was calling rugby league on TV while I was doing my best on the field of play. He was always kind to me in commentary. At one point in my career, Ray gave me two man-of-the-match awards in a row on consecutive Sunday afternoons. I think the prizes were $500 cash and a Meapro ham.

A week later I ran into him at the races, and he boomed at me – so loudly that everyone could hear – 'I've given you two man-of-the-match awards in two weeks, and you haven't even offered me a slice of ham!'

I invited Ray and his lady over to my place for a barbeque the following week, and we've been great mates ever since.

Ray is neurotic, emotional, paranoid, sensitive, over-reactive and anxious. But he still makes me laugh. He used to be so sensitive to any criticism of his commentary that he genuinely feared making a mistake. He is far more relaxed about it these days, because he's heard Peter Sterling or Fatty Vautin or me making ten times as many mistakes as he could ever make.

He used to worry about what was written in the newspapers. He would ring me in a panic on a Sunday morning and say, 'Did you read this thing in the paper today? Are they talking about me?'

'No, Ray,' I'd reply. 'I didn't, mate. What does it say?'

He would read me the offending article, and I would assure him it had nothing to do with him and that it was about someone else.

'Oh,' he'd say. 'That's okay, then.' And off he'd go. Problem averted.

He is a hypochondriac – the worst I have ever encountered. He's had so many illnesses, ailments, conditions, sicknesses, and he's experienced so many cures, medications, treatments, surgeries, procedures and lotions, that he could actually pass a doctor's exam. He diagnoses everyone he meets. He knows exactly what ails you because, as he says, he has had the same thing himself.

I mean it. He is a walking, talking chemist. He has a medical cabinet in his bag wherever he goes. He has his doctor on speed dial.

Ray has always hated flying. He was much worse years ago, though. I actually think that, these days, he has become a lot calmer about taking to the skies. Mind you, just before take-off on every flight, he always texts his lovely wife, Cher, to tell her he loves her, and to say goodbye. Goodbye! Fancy having to travel with this pessimist everywhere we go!

Ray genuinely hates being away from home. He loves his family and hates to travel without them. At work, he is at his happiest when his family has travelled with him.

His pet obsession is planning his getaway from the football ground after the full-time siren to beat the traffic, to get the earlier flight, to get home a little sooner. His strategising starts the Monday before we travel. He organises the best parking spot, closest to the exit gate, with the car's nose pointing in the right direction. If the car park is too far away, Ray has been known to arrange a game-day official in a golf cart to drive us quickly to our cars.

If you ever hear Ray giving a complimentary mention to the local school across the road from the football ground where we are calling, chances are he is parked in the principal's private car spot at the front of the building.

Ray even organises his travel route to and from the stadium. On big nights in Brisbane when they're expecting a big crowd at Suncorp Stadium, the surrounding streets are blocked off by the police to control the traffic flow. Every car has to approach and leave by the same roads.

Not my Ray. He'll contact the local traffic command and organise to be let past the road barriers. As we approach each roadblock he'll say to me, 'This bloke's name is John.' Then he winds down the window as we approach, sticks his head out the window and, with a big smile, says, 'Hi, John, I'm Ray Warren.'

Traffic controller John immediately springs into action and pulls back the roadblock so we can pass up the empty street ahead. 'Have a great call, Ray,' John will yell as Ray waves him thanks and goodbye. What I later learnt was that at the end of each season all these blokes get a carton of their favourite beverage, courtesy of the appreciative Mr Warren. He thinks of everything.

When we travel interstate, Ray always organises the best room, in the best hotel, at the best rate. I now let Ray handle all our travel arrangements. I just follow behind.

Anyway, enough of the stories. Let's get serious for a moment, because I really want the last impression you get of Ray from this book to be the most accurate. Make no mistake, Ray 'Rabbits' Warren, born on 11 June 1943 – sporting commentator, TV personality, radio host, master of ceremonies, entertainer – is a legend in Australian sport.

Ray is the complete professional. He takes great pride in his work. It has been the greatest learning experience of my life to work with this extraordinary man on many platforms.

His distinctive and descriptive turn of phrase is unique. His ability to raise his voice, almost screaming, but not miss a name or a pronunciation always leaves me in awe. He has a wonderful grasp of what he calls 'light and shade'. The tempo of his commentary mirrors the tempo of the action being played out before him. He can go from calm and controlled to frantic and loud within an instant. It's brilliant.

Ray has the wonderful quality of knowing the art of entertainment. He knows what people want to hear. His voice rises with the sound of the crowd. He will argue the point to create theatre. He wants the people listening to his opinions to think about and react to what he says. He performs for them. He wants them to enjoy the work he is presenting.

He unselfishly gives of himself in his media work. He willingly and regularly donates his time and expertise to charitable events and fundraisers. Ray is a wonderful host. His interviews are insightful. He probes with his questions, looking to get a reaction from the subject. He asks the questions he thinks the people listening want answered.

Ray stops to talk to everyone. He doesn't just pose for photographs or sign autographs; he stops and has a conversation with the person making the request. After a brief conversation, he'll know which town they came from, and invariably he'll know someone that they know from their home town.

He remembers people's names. He is personable, kind and complimentary with everyone he meets. You might run into him again twelve months later and he will call you by name.

And, of course, his football commentary is second to none.

I think back to when I was coaching my last State of

Origin match for New South Wales, back in season 2004. We were coming into a series decider at ANZ Stadium in Sydney. As our team bus turned into the tunnel under the stadium, I put on a DVD for the players. It was simply vision of every player in our team doing something great on the football field. I intended it as positive mental reinforcement of their talents, and I hoped it would raise their confidence and self-belief.

As the tape rolled on, the players' eyes were fixed on the screen. I soon noticed, though, that it wasn't the vision that was attracting our attention. It was the sound. It was Ray's familiar and booming voice.

One by one, Ray called the name of each player on that bus as he did something special in a recent game. *'Gasnier! Brilliant! . . . Fittler does it again! . . . Look at this man Barrett! . . . Mason is a man mountain!'* On and on he went. And as his voice rose, I could feel the mood of our players rise.

It's not the vision that sells this game. It's not just the amazing feats of these mighty players. It's the way Ray calls the action. The sense of theatre he brings to the call. It inspired these great players. It lifted them.

I'm not saying that was the reason New South Wales won that decider in 2004. But I do know it had a definite effect on the players' psyches as they entered the final period of preparation.

I believe Ray has been selling rugby league for decades. He makes the game better. He brings the game to life in lounge rooms all over the country.

Kids in the playground mimic his voice as they play touch footy with their mates. That's influence.

Ray Warren is the voice of rugby league. There will never be another Ray Warren.

Phil Gould
April 2014

St Vincent's Prostate Cancer Centre is a centre dedicated to research, education and awareness of prostate cancer, and to improving the quality of care of patients with prostate cancer. Directed by Professor Phillip Stricker, it works in association with the Garvan Institute, the Kinghorn Cancer Centre and the Australian Prostate Cancer Research Centre, New South Wales. Its research is in the diagnosis, treatment and management of patients with localised and advanced prostate cancer. Prostate cancer continues to be a major health issue among Australian men: a new diagnosis of prostate cancer occurs in 20,000 men a year, and 3000 men lose their lives to the disease each year. The aim of the centre is to decrease the impact of prostate cancer on Australian men.

FOR MORE INFORMATION, VISIT WWW.PROSTATE.COM.AU

Lightning Source UK Ltd.
Milton Keynes UK
UKOW06n2335141014

240082UK00001B/2/P

9 781863 956758